"The more I learned about God's goodness, the more I realized how little I truly trusted Him. I asked God to use the teaching to transform my mind. He answered those prayers and established a firm foundation of trust in His goodness. Without this understanding, which developed through a day-by-day walk with Jesus through joys and deep sorrows, I would remain stuck in the early stages of spiritual transformation. The fruit of knowing God's goodness in the depths of my soul brings peace and intimacy with my Creator. This rest has brought calm into my life, and I no longer feel the need to perform for the approval of God or others. Instead of losing myself in Christ, I am finding the person God created me to be."

— LINDA STROHKORB, mother of three teenagers

"Drawing upon their rich life experiences and deep passion for God, authors Mimi Wilson and Shelly Cook Volkhardt explore the essence of God's character and attributes. By examining God as the physical source of light, the essence of truth, the creator of time, and the source of all goodness, Mimi and Shelly unfold doctrinal truths in a manner both approachable and profound. With expertise from years of intimately looking at God's holiness, they shine fresh light on the richness of God's character so the reader's vision of God becomes sharper and clearer."

— PEGGY LANUM, mother of two grade-school children

mimi wilson and shelly cook volkhardt

trusting in **His goodness**

a woman's guide to knowing God's purpose

NAVPRESS

NAVPRESS○

NavPress is the publishing ministry of The Navigators, an international Christian organization and leader in personal spiritual development. NavPress is committed to helping people grow spiritually and enjoy lives of meaning and hope through personal and group resources that are biblically rooted, culturally relevant, and highly practical.

For a free catalog go to www.NavPress.com
or call 1.800.366.7788 in the United States or 1.800.839.4769 in Canada.

© 2010 by Shelly Cook Volkhardt and Mimi Wilson

All rights reserved. No part of this publication may be reproduced in any form without written permission from NavPress, P.O. Box 35001, Colorado Springs, CO 80935. www.navpress.com

ISBN: 978-1-60006-715-0

Cover design by Gearbox
Cover image by Masterfile

Some of the anecdotal illustrations in this book are true to life and are included with the permission of the persons involved. All other illustrations are composites of real situations, and any resemblance to people living or dead is coincidental.

Library of Congress Cataloging-in-Publication Data

Wilson, Mimi, 1946-
  Trusting in His goodness : a woman's guide to knowing God's purpose / Mimi Wilson and Shelly Cook Volkhardt.
    p. cm.
  Includes bibliographical references.
  ISBN 978-1-60006-715-0
  1. God (Christianity)--Goodness. 2. Trust in God--Christianity. I. Volkhardt, Shelly Cook. II. Title.
  BT137.W55 2010
  248.8'43--dc22
                                2009037814

Printed in the United States of America

1 2 3 4 5 6 7 8 / 14 13 12 11 10

From Mimi:

To my dear husband, Cal; to our children, Kurt and
Lori, Tom and Kyndra, Kevin and Sarah; and to my
precious grandchildren, whom I love dearly.

From Shelly:

For my precious "boys" — Glen, my beloved; Carl;
and Culver — with deep love and thanks to God
for the family He has made us.

For Mimi and the other women who have built
into my life by their example, teaching, and friend-
ship; you have enriched me forever.

For Dad, Mom, and my sister, Milei — this book
and this life would not be the same without
all you have taught me.

Contents

Acknowledgments 9

Chapter 1   360 Degrees of Absolute Goodness 11

Chapter 2   Out from Behind the Curtain 25

Chapter 3   Dancing in Life-Giving Light 41

Chapter 4   Swept Off Your Feet 61

Chapter 5   Guilt-Free and Spiritually Whole 77

Chapter 6   Radiant with Joy 97

Chapter 7   Becoming One 111

Chapter 8   Trusting in His Grip 127

Chapter 9   Beyond "Till Death Do Us Part" 141

Chapter 10   Shipwrecks Turned Gorgeous Coral Reefs 157

Chapter 11   Expecting Him to Show Up 173

Chapter 12   Enjoying His Rest 187

Notes 197

About the Authors 203

Acknowledgments

To Liz: Your role as editor has deeply enriched the way we present truth! We have learned so much from you and are forever grateful for your valuable guidance and insights.

Deep thanks for above-and-beyond contributions of time, energy, life stories, thoughts, research, and writing to: Glen Volkhardt, Cal Wilson, Milei Yardley, Kent Wilson, Linda Dillow, Karen Doerksen and the women of Northeast Bible Chapel, Jack Harrison, John and Barb Odom, Ed Murphy, Beth Wahl, Carol-Lyn Davis, Margaret Gowan, Anita Becdach, Becky Sims, Leslie Kerrigan, DaVinda Hsu, Shannon Wingrove, Julie Witt, Rick and Jo Jackson, Karl Bruce, our friends at Camp Elim (for providing a writing getaway), Norm and Muriel Cook, Hope Anderson, Verna Narwold, Alice Tate, Donna Pease, and Mrs. Moss.

For prayer support and encouragement: Beth Travis, Lois Vos, Nancy Mlakar, Ruth Craig and the Hope of the Harvest team, Liz and Brian Cox and the Valley Church missionary prayer team, our Paraclete colleagues, the "Hands and Feet of Jesus" care group from Mountain Springs Church, and our "mentor girls."

Chapter 1

360 Degrees of Absolute Goodness

Karen welcomed us warmly as we stepped into her lovely home. Windows two stories tall looked out onto breathtaking mountains wearing white winter hats of snow. The sun was shining with a brilliance defying the bitter cold. The dining table was perfectly set, and Karen served us a delicious meal. She seemed to enjoy a fairy-tale existence: She had a handsome, successful husband and a beautiful son who made top honors at school and excelled on the basketball team. But when we asked her if she had other children, something indefinable flitted across her face.

"We have a daughter in heaven," she said. "Two years ago our Katie died. She was a few weeks shy of her university graduation. We were stunned when we got the news. We couldn't believe it when the police ruled it a suicide. The grief was suffocating, overwhelming. We couldn't comprehend any of it. Katie's boyfriend was as shocked as we were. Like us, he had no inkling Katie was heavyhearted. Her professors described her as a dedicated student, intelligent, bright, and happy. No one in our daughter's life could have imagined that she would take her life.

"I was angry at God. How could He let Katie commit suicide? Why didn't He make us aware of her despondency? If she was murdered, why hadn't He protected her? Doesn't the Bible say that God protects His children? Katie loved God; she had committed her life to Him. She had so much to offer Him, and now she was gone. Most days I could barely breathe through the horror of it. I was teetering on the conclusion that God was at fault, that He must not really be a good God if He would let Katie die, regardless of how it happened."

Is God Really Good?

Karen wanted to know, *Is God really good? Can I trust Him?* We don't know anyone who hasn't asked these questions, who at some point hasn't wondered if God didn't have it out for them. The problem is, many people never get beyond the questions; they remain stuck in their doubts.

Without a strong confidence in God's goodness, it's impossible to build a foundation from which we can cultivate gratefulness, trust, obedience, and rest, which lead to transformation. If we don't believe that God is good, we will become cynical and angry when difficulties come our way. If we don't believe He is good, we can't trust Him with all of our life, we can't obey Him in everything, and we can't give thanks for the hard things in life. Transformation — Christlikeness — comes as we live within the circle of God's goodness, viewing everything that happens through that lens. When we live in the circle of God's goodness, it becomes the filter for how we interpret everything in life — the good and the bad, the beautiful and the horrific.

Even the first woman wondered if God was good. When Satan approached Eve in the Garden of Eden, he asked a question that got her to focus on the fruit of the forbidden tree. She began to wonder, *If God is good, why would He forbid me to eat something that is good for me?*

What if Eve's answer to the serpent's question had been, "Look to the east. As far as your eye can see, I can eat of the fruit of any tree. Look to the west. As far as your eye can see, I can eat of the fruit of any tree. To the north and south, the same. Why would I sit under the tree and focus on the fruit I cannot have?" Like Eve's, our eyes are often on the things that God has determined are not for our benefit. Being finite, Eve could not understand God's ways, nor can we.

What would Eve have seen if instead of focusing on the fruit that God said she could not have she had looked around at His provision? The trees were newly created, and the fruit was surely the best of the best, the colors deep, rich, and inviting. There was likely every variety of apricots, apples, pears, kiwis, plums, oranges, lemons, pomegranates, watermelons, strawberries, and so much more. Eve was surrounded by a 360-degree panorama of God's abundant goodness, but her focus was locked in on what she could not have. If she had fixated on what God did permit, she would have been able to put the forbidden fruit into perspective even though she did not grasp God's purposes. If Eve had only paid attention to God's bounty, how different the outcome of her life would have been! And how dramatically changed our lives could be if we did the same.

Few of us know what it is to live in the circle of God's goodness. We may understand intellectually that God is good, and we may even have stepped into a slice of His goodness, but our focus is typically on only one or two aspects of it: on His sovereignty or on His love. Like Eve, we often look to what we don't have and decide (many times without realizing it) that God must not be good since we cannot have what we desire. We don't have to look far to see evidence of this. Single women bemoan that they have no husband, and married women wish they didn't have the husbands they have. Chronically ill women grieve over being sick. Childless women mourn their infertility, and those who have children weep over yet another pregnancy. Some women wish they were skinnier, and others wish they were fatter, and on it goes.

It's not wrong to feel sadness and grief over these things. It's normal. However, when these feelings dominate our lives, we're tempted to focus on the negatives and allow them to grow so big in our minds that they blot out all the good. Consequently, we miss the essence of who God is.

God's Essence

Everything good in the world is born out of God's character. All that is good comes from Him. We can see goodness in a myriad of things in our daily lives — in the fresh bloom of a rose, the loving smile of a friend, the innocence of a newborn baby, and the gifts of taste, movement, and smell. And in life itself. The essence of goodness, its true flavor, comes from God because He *is* goodness.

Moses saw God in ways that were unknown before his day. He encountered God at the burning bush. He witnessed the plagues in Egypt and stood on the banks of the Red Sea as the waters parted. He camped under smoke coming from Mt. Sinai, yet he still asked for further insight into God's character. He experienced the presence of God, but still he longed for more. In Exodus 33:18, Moses makes a simple request: "Now show me your glory."

Graciously God replies,

I will cause all my goodness to pass in front of you, and I will proclaim my name, the LORD, in your presence. I will have mercy on whom I will have mercy, and I will have compassion on whom I will have compassion. You cannot see my face, for no one may see me and live. (Exodus 33:19-20)

Then He adds,

There is a place near me where you may stand on a rock. When my glory passes by, I will put you in a cleft in the rock and cover you with my hand until I have passed by. Then I will remove my hand and you will see my back; but my face must not be seen. (verses 21-23)

When Moses asks to see God's glory, God responds by offering to show His goodness. Why would He do that? Because every facet of the expansive character of God is partnered with His goodness. God's goodness is so much more than the glory Moses wanted to see. He was asking for a slice when God wanted Him to see a bigger picture. Goodness is "His essence."[1]

In this event, God clearly tied His name to His goodness. The name *Lord* can be translated Jehovah or "I AM that I AM." This was the same name God used when He introduced Himself to Moses at the burning bush. As the I AM, God's goodness is self-existent and eternal, always in the present. It is unchanging. Out of His goodness, He created all things and maintains all things. His good rule is absolutely sovereign.

When God speaks to Moses in this passage, He displays His goodness through acts of mercy and compassion. We see His mercy as He prepares Moses for the encounter. He tells Moses that man cannot look on Him and live, so He finds a rock for Moses to hide behind when He reveals Himself. We see His compassion when He covers Moses with His hand. Who is God protecting Moses from? From Himself! How little we understand this. Nothing created can protect us from the consuming holiness of almighty God. Moses would have died unless he was hidden *in* God from the consuming power *of* God. Only the uncreated hand of God could keep Moses alive. There was no safer place in the universe for Moses to be.

The same is true for us. Just as Moses would have died by looking directly at God, so would we. God's hand still must protect us from His consuming holiness. But we can see even more of God's goodness in that the hand that covers us is pierced. We cannot draw near to God unless He makes it possible. Jesus Christ's death on the cross covers our sins. This covering allows us to draw near to God without fear of death. Moses saw God's revelation of Himself through the protection of God's hand. We can look at our world and our circumstances through His nail-pierced hand.

The next day when Moses goes to meet with God,

The LORD came down in the cloud and stood there with him and proclaimed his name, the LORD. And he passed in front of Moses, proclaiming, "The LORD, the LORD, the compassionate and gracious God, slow to anger, abounding in love and faithfulness, maintaining love to thousands, and forgiving wickedness, rebellion and sin." (Exodus 34:5-7)

As Moses hides in the rock, covered by God's hand, he hears further declarations of God's goodness. He first announces Himself as the Lord. This is a reminder to Moses that He is transcendent, above all created and uncreated. He tells Moses that He is compassionate, full of tender affection toward Moses and all His people. His graciousness indicates the manner in which He gives all His gifts. He longs to show kindness instead of rushing to anger. Out of His abundant goodness and faithfulness He shows His love, and despite His complete holiness, He forgives wickedness, rebellion, and sin (see Exodus 34:6-7). Each revelation shows more of God's goodness. As He passed before Moses, He passes in front of us day by day to allow us a better view of who He is.

Paul, in Ephesians 3:18-19, prays that we would grasp the infinite dimensions of God's character. His goodness is limitless because His resources are limitless, and it is infinite — without end — because He is infinite. The psalmist wrote, "The eyes of all look to you, and you give them their food at the proper time. You open your hand and satisfy the desires of every living thing" (Psalm 145:15-16). God can meet the needs of everything living at the same time and not deplete the amount of goodness in His own being.

This is hard for us to grasp. We all have limitations, and because of this we often unknowingly project those boundaries onto God. When we come to Him and ask for more of His goodness, He doesn't turn

His pockets inside out and say, "I'm all out; there's no more left." His goodness is never-ending; we cannot make a dent in it. If all mankind had a cup and could dip it into the goodness of God's character at the same time, our cups would be full and He would not have a drop less of goodness in Him. When we project limits onto God and His goodness, we make Him into a little god in our own image.

God's goodness is for all and is seen by all, not just a few chosen ones. Matthew 5:45 says, "He causes his sun to rise on the evil and the good, and sends rain on the righteous and the unrighteous." No one lives without evidence of God's goodness. Since the creation of the world, God has made Himself plainly known through what He created. He revealed His nature — His goodness as well as the rest of who He is — through creation. "Since the creation of the world God's invisible qualities — his eternal power and divine nature — have been clearly seen, being understood from what has been made" (Romans 1:20). What we know of God can point the way for us to keep moving toward Him.

If we look at creation and fail to see the Creator, we are no different from the people Paul talked about in Romans 1:21-22: "Although they knew God, they neither glorified him as God nor gave thanks to him, but their thinking became futile and their foolish hearts were darkened. Although they claimed to be wise, they became fools." At best, we limit ourselves to a small slice of the whole pie of the goodness of God. The people of whom Paul wrote didn't allow themselves to recognize God's hand, which led them into further darkness and depravity. One translation of verse 25 says that they suppressed the truth.[2] It was not ignorance on their part; it was rebellion. The result was that they ended up worshipping creation or idols — the work of their own hands — instead of their Creator God. The goodness of God was all around them, but they denied it.

When we don't pay attention to the goodness of God surrounding us, we starve our belief that God is good and weaken its foundation.

When that happens and the storms of life batter us, our foundation cracks and we blame God and question His goodness.

How can we become more aware of God's goodness? It's simple, really.

The Art of Savoring His Goodness

The first step to noticing God's goodness is opening our eyes and looking for it.

Shelly:

The backyard of our first home ended in a lake. It was a draw for birds of all kinds. Our first few weeks there, Glen kept saying to me, "Did you see that bird?" He would then describe the color of the bird's beak, wingtips, sometimes even his feet. I was surprised by the details he could give me. To me a bird was a bird. I had never stopped to notice coloring, markings, and physical characteristics.

I bought Glen a bird book and a pair of binoculars for his birthday and we decided to become students of the birds of South Florida. I learned to identify the egrets that came to feed on the fish in the shallow water, the blue heron that flew onto the neighbor's deck across the lake, the sand hill cranes oddly standing in the grass of a field, and many others. A new world opened up to me, all because we decided to cultivate an awareness of the birds of South Florida.

For years I was blind to the evidence of God's goodness all around me the same way I was to birds. I was numb to the circle of His goodness; I allowed it to simply be a part of the scenery, nothing remarkable. I never paid attention.

When the psalmist said, "Taste and see that the LORD is good" (Psalm 34:8), he was telling us to use our senses to pay attention to the world God created. When we do, we expand our awareness of His goodness.

Many times when we eat we don't pay attention to how the food tastes or how it looks. Contrast this approach with that of professional wine tasters. They pay careful attention to the wine sample in front of them. They hold the glass in their hands and carefully watch how the liquid slides down the sides of the glass. They sniff the wine to capture subtle aromas. They roll the wine around in their mouth, exposing it to all their taste buds. They pay attention to the wine's texture and how it feels. Once they swallow the wine, they note its aftertaste. How long does it last? Do they like the taste? Savoring is an art. It requires time, practice, and focus.

God has given us innumerable spices, colors, and textures to savor. He could have made everything in black and white, but He made food with brilliant colors. The skin of a single mango, for example, can have green, yellow, orange, and even red in it. Each time we notice these things, we can choose to look up into God's face and express our pleasure at His goodness in giving us such a rich variety. As we do this, we strengthen the foundation of our faith in His goodness. The more we store up evidence of His goodness, the stronger our resolve will be to trust Him when our circumstances tempt us to doubt Him.

I Have Resolved . . .

Barbi grew up the youngest of six children. A few days before her birthday, she hugged her father good-bye before he went on a hunting trip. It was the last hug she ever got from him. The next time she saw her dad, on her birthday, he was lying in a casket. Barbi says her dad was bigger than life. He swept everyone up in his expansive enjoyment and passion for life. The emptiness she felt after his death was devastating. After her father's funeral, she told God, "If You exist, You are going to have to reveal Yourself to me. I want to know You."

The following year, some youth leaders from a nearby church reached out to Barbi during a visit to the school lunchroom. They began to teach her about a personal relationship with Jesus Christ. Barbi fell passionately in love with Him and grew quickly in her faith. She couldn't get enough of God's goodness, love, and care for her.

In college she met John, who was deeply in love with God and pursuing His ways, and they eventually married. However, when her husband was in medical school, he began to make some ungodly decisions. They had two small children when Barbi discovered he was having an affair. During those wilderness days, Barbi kept reminding herself that God is good, even when her situation wasn't. She asked God to be her "manna" for the moment. For years she affirmed God's goodness, staying faithful and praying for John. In time, his heart came home to God and to Barbi. They had two more children, whom she refers to as Mercy and Grace, fruit after a barren time of the soul.

The financial pressures of medical school loans and providing for a growing family kept John working night and day in the hospital emergency room. One day, her mother told Barbi, "You're just worn out. You need a vacation. I'm going to take you and the children to Florida for a week." Grateful and exhausted, she climbed on the plane with her mother, her sister Jodi, and all four children.

When they reached cruising altitude, Barbi noticed that Gabbie, her two-year-old, had spiked a fever. Then she began to convulse. Holding Gabbie, Barbi called out, "Is there a doctor on the plane? We need a doctor." In response, an elderly physician made his way up the aisle. As Gabbie continued to seize, Barbi held her little girl, who represented the fresh love and new life in her marriage. Passengers hovered. Gabbie convulsed for more than thirty minutes before the pilot was able to make an emergency landing. An ambulance met the plane on the airfield, and paramedics worked on the little girl. When Gabbie woke up, the doctors told Barbi that her daughter had miraculously suffered no mental loss or brain damage.

Later Barbi's sister asked her, "What does it mean that you have resolved God is good?" When Barbi asked what she meant, Jodi went on to tell her that while all the passengers were standing, watching the event, "between fifty and hundred times you repeated, 'Sweet baby, don't leave me, but I have *resolved* God is good.'" Barbi had no recollection of saying these words, but she knew what they meant.

Long before the crisis with Gabbie, Barbi had chosen to stand on what she knew to be true about God, regardless of her circumstances. His goodness had become part of the fabric of who she was and what she believed. When faced with a fresh crisis, she unconsciously resorted to what she knew to be true of God. She lives in the circle of God's goodness.

Wouldn't you like to do the same?

What's Ahead

For the last ten years, the two of us have immersed ourselves in knowing the goodness of God. This book is a summary of what we have learned and shared with each other along the way. Throughout the following chapters, we will look at some aspects of God's goodness and how you can savor and embrace each of them. You will see how He transforms us into women who can rest in the circle of His absolute goodness, whether we're living in an oasis or a desert.

In our first book, *Holy Habits*, we wrote about some spiritual practices that have become an integral part of our walk with God, and we've done the same here.

Shelly:

Soon after we moved back to the United States after living twenty years in Latin America, my hair began to fall out. I found hair in the shower, in the sink, and on the floor. Every time I swept my hair off the tile floor in our new home, I worried about becoming bald. Then one day as I was sweeping up my hairs, I remembered Matthew 10:30, "Even the very hairs of your head are all numbered." Suddenly

I realized that God knows how many hairs I have left! What incred-
ible goodness and love, that He would care about something so insig-
nificant when the entire universe is under His watchful eye.

As the immenseness of God's loving goodness washed over me, I
realized that I could use my hair loss as a trigger for a holy habit: I
decided that every time I found a hair, I would remind myself that
He knows how many hairs are left on my head and breathe a prayer
of thanks for His amazing goodness and love. As I practiced that
holy habit, my focus shifted from the loss of my hair to the One whose
goodness surrounds me.

We've discovered that the choice to cultivate a holy habit usually
takes no more time — probably less — than the worry and preoccupa-
tion we can allow ourselves to fall into. At the end of each chapter, we
have included some holy habits that can help you pay attention to God
and His goodness. The first is a verse of Scripture we encourage you to
memorize. In addition, choose at least one holy habit and practice it
daily. (Don't try to do them all.) We also encourage you to answer the
study questions that go along with each chapter.

Like Moses, we have cried, "Show me your glory!" Is this your
heart cry as well? Join us as we seek to learn to live ever more fully in the
circle of God's goodness.

Good Savior, as we embark on this study, help us grow to recognize Your
abundant goodness surrounding us. Teach us how to live. We don't want to
miss what You want to do in our lives. We long to become so aware of Your
goodness that even in our subconscious it is the bedrock we stand on when we
face the storms of life. Thank You for making Your circle of goodness avail-
able to us.

Holy Habits

- Verse to memorize: "Taste and see that the LORD is good; blessed is the man who takes refuge in him" (Psalm 34:8).

- When you eat, deliberately take a second to let yourself savor the flavor of the food and thank Him for His goodness in giving you taste. "Taste and see" (Psalm 34:8).

- Every time you lose a hair, thank God for His goodness in keeping track of every single one on your head.

- Resolve that God is good. When you are tempted to focus on what you can't have or don't have, look around at what you do have. Thank Him, with your will, for all the things that He has given you.

Responding to His Word

1. Everybody is tempted to question God's goodness. How have you done that?
2. In Exodus 33:18, Moses asked God to show him His glory. God's reply was that He would pass His goodness before Moses. Where do you see God's glory in His goodness in your life?
3. Psalm 72:19 says that the "earth [is] filled with his glory," and Psalm 33:5 tells us that the "earth is full of the goodness of the LORD" (KJV). Do you see His glory/goodness anywhere in recent natural disasters that have taken place? Make a list of what comes to mind and thank God for those things as He points them out to you.
4. Read Exodus 33:19-22 and 34:5-7. Note that in chapter 33, God announces what He is going to show Moses and then shows him in chapter 34. List what those verses tell you about who God is.

5. Read the list of characteristics God revealed to Moses. Note which is the easiest and which is the most challenging for you to believe is a part of His goodness.

6. What can you do to cultivate an awareness of God's goodness? Glen and Shelly got a book to learn more about birds. What can you use as guides to become more aware of His goodness?

7. Meditate on the following words from an ancient hymn. How do you think God's goodness and the other aspects of His character can "bind" our hearts to Him?

> *"Let Thy goodness like a fetter*
>   *Bind my wandering heart to Thee"*[3]

8. The psalmist says that we can experience the goodness of God through our senses. Psalm 34:8 calls us to taste and see that the Lord is good. How might you "taste" the goodness of God? Write a prayer asking God to open each of your senses to His goodness.

9. Write a resolution regarding what you choose to believe about God. Put it in a prominent place and declare it regularly as a reminder.

10. How do you respond to the description of holy habits? Are there things you do already that could be called holy habits? Do you know of things that other people do to remind them of God's character? What are they?

Chapter 2

Out from Behind the Curtain

Years ago Mimi visited a wealthy woman in South America whose home was full of priceless Asian antiques. When she asked how her friend had acquired them, she heard an interesting story.

Mimi:

My friend had grown up in Paraguay and told me that before the Second World War, her father was the Paraguayan ambassador to Japan. The Japanese emperor wanted to establish a trade agreement with Paraguay, so he summoned her father for an audience and the family traveled by ship to Japan. The voyage lasted more than a month. They went through several storms, and the tossing and turning that ensued made them seasick. When they finally arrived at their destination, a group of Japanese schoolchildren met them at the dock and welcomed them with songs. Then the entire family was taken on a tour of Japan as honored guests of the emperor. They had yet to meet him.

Everyone in the family anticipated the day when their father would finally be able to accomplish the purpose of his trip and meet with the emperor. When the day came, her father carefully prepared for the occasion. He polished his shoes and had his clothes carefully cleaned and pressed. When he arrived at the palace, dressed in his top hat, tails, and gloves, the officials instructed him to enter the emperor's throne room, bow to a curtain, and quickly leave. That was it!

When my friend finished her story, I asked, "Didn't your father see the emperor? What did he look like? How was he dressed? Did he speak to your father?"

"Oh no," she replied. "It was forbidden for an ordinary person to look at the emperor." She went on to tell me that at that time, the Japanese considered the emperor to be a god. As she began to show me all the beautiful Japanese things they had acquired on their long journey, I wondered what would have happened if the ambassador had just reached out and opened the curtain.

Can you imagine traveling for that long and over such a long distance only to bow to a curtain? To not ever see or meet the person who had summoned you for an audience? What a letdown to an enormous amount of effort and build up! The only way the ambassador would have ever met the emperor would have been for the emperor to have come out and shown himself. As the supreme ruler of the country, the emperor could have done whatever he wanted, including breaking any taboos. He even could have gone to the trouble of taking the long journey from Japan to Paraguay, but that would have put him on the same level as the people he ruled over. By summoning the ambassador to come to him, the emperor was rightfully asserting his power and greatness.

What a difference between how God treats us and how the emperor treated the ambassador! The restrictive ancient code for the Japanese emperor was isolation, yet God's loving eternal code is revelation. The only way that we can possibly know God — and His goodness — is if He reveals Himself to us. And He has! He has shown us His goodness through His intricately created world, through His beloved Son (the embodied Word), and through inspired Scripture (the written Word).

God, like the emperor, could have remained hidden from us. But in His goodness, He broke the silence of eternity and created the universe so that we could get to know Him.

We See His Goodness in Creation

Nine times in Genesis 1 it says that in creation, "God said" and it was so. God spoke the world into being, and His creation reflects who He is. Creation continues to speak, revealing God to all who will listen:

> *The heavens declare the glory of God;*
> *the skies proclaim the work of his hands.*
> *Day after day they pour forth speech;*
> *night after night they display knowledge.*
> *There is no speech or language*
> *where their voice is not heard. (Psalm 19:1-3)*

With the act of creation, God pulled back the curtain of unknowing and stepped through, not only so that we could get a better look at Him but also so we could have relationship with Him. He created the earth as an expression of who He is.

Shelly:

The summer I turned thirteen, I experienced God as the Lover of my soul. In an attempt to make Him a part of my everyday life, I had made a commitment to look for Him in everything. Our family was on a long car trip, and my little sister and I were doing our share of backseat bickering. Since the imaginary line we had drawn wasn't working, our daddy finally put a suitcase between us. We were hot and sweaty because our car had no air conditioner. I read my book until car sickness drove me to stare out the window.

As I looked at the countryside hurtling past, I asked, "God, where are You in all this?" Suddenly everything took on a sparkly quality. My heart started beating faster as I realized that God was revealing Himself to me in His creation. With my newly opened eyes, I was struck with God's attention to detail as revealed in tiny, delicate flowers blowing in the wind, in intricate designs on the backs of lizards sunning themselves, and in multicolored layers of rock folding back on themselves in artistic swirls. As I gazed at the grandeur of the enormous mountains standing against a backdrop of deep blue sky, flattened plateaus, and huge boulders resting on almost nothing, I got a glimpse of God's greatness, beauty, and power. I was so overwhelmed with the wonder of His artistry, order, and perfection I had to shut my eyes.

I felt overwhelmed with the knowledge that the One who had spoken into being everything I saw outside the car window had made me as well! I was stunned into an awed silence (a rare occurrence). This almighty, good God had revealed Himself — to me personally! How He must love me to go to such lengths!

Most of us don't think about what God's creation reveals about Him. We take it for granted or become calloused to it. When that happens, we unhook ourselves from Him. But God takes pleasure in showing Himself to us through creation. "He made known to us the mystery of his will *according to his good pleasure*" (Ephesians 1:9, emphasis added). He wants us to know Him, and He delights in showing Himself to us.

God did not have to reveal Himself to us. He certainly didn't need to. He was perfectly complete. That He did so underscores His goodness. He did it for us because He loves us.

When God looked at His work, He saw that "it was very good" (Genesis 1:31). Creation shouts the goodness of God, but it is up to us to notice it. When we study the intricate requirements for maintaining life on earth — the golden tone of an aspen leaf in fall, a lacy tropical fern drenched in sunlight, the tiny purple bags of juice we call grapes — we can only conclude that the Mind that thought it up and the Heart that made it known is good.

God did not set creation into motion and then step back from what He made. He keeps it all going. "The Son [Jesus Christ] is . . . sustaining all things by his powerful word" (Hebrews 1:3). We see this in the regularity of spring, summer, fall, and winter; in day changing into night and back to day; and in the tide coming in and going out over the earth. "God is the God of life Who sustains all, but Who is Himself independent of all. He gives to all, but He is enriched by none."[1]

When people tell us that they don't see God working in their lives, we say, "The breath you just took shows that God is at work in you. If He did not sustain your life, you wouldn't be able to take in air. You would be dead!" Every breath we take is an example of the good and ongoing work of God (see Acts 17:25).

When God starts something in us, He *will* finish it. It is part of who He is. "He who has begun a good work . . . will complete it" (Philippians 1:6, NKJV). God not only created us, He sustains us. As He sustains us, He is also carrying us forward toward godliness. That principle is underlined in Isaiah 55:11:

> *My word that goes out from my mouth:*
> *It will not return to me empty,*
> *but will accomplish what I desire*
> *and achieve the purpose for which I sent it.*

If creation tells us so much of the mind of God, how much more does the person of Christ, "the radiance of God's glory and the exact representation of his being" (Hebrews 1:3), reveal about Him?

We Can See His Goodness in His Son

God's goodness is embodied in His Son, Jesus Christ, the Word:

> *In the beginning was the Word, and the Word was with God, and the Word was God. He was with God in the beginning. Through him all things were made; without him nothing was made that has been made. . . . The Word became flesh and made his dwelling among us. We have seen his glory, the glory of the One and Only, who came from the Father, full of grace and truth. (John 1:1-3,14)*

In Greek, the word *dwelling* is the same word used for tabernacle or tent. In sending His son to earth to live among us, God pitched His tent with us. He did not have to come and live among us, but He chose to do so anyway. God's love and goodness motivated Him to humble Himself so that He might bridge the gap between Himself and us. When Christ came to earth, He fulfilled the plan that God had conceived before the beginning of time. God identified with us in our humanity and did not sequester Himself behind the curtain of His holiness. Through His Son, He stepped out from behind that barrier. He revealed Himself and His desire for relationship with us.

When Jesus' disciples asked Him to show God to them, He replied, "Anyone who has seen me has seen the Father" (John 14:9). Throughout the Gospels, God illustrates His heart through His Son. For example:

- When Jesus asked blind Bartimaeus, "What do you want me to do for you?" (Mark 10:51), He showed us that God wants to know what is on our hearts.
- When He brought the widow's only son back to life, Jesus unveiled God's tender compassion and understanding. "When

the Lord saw her, his heart went out to her and he said, 'Don't cry'" (Luke 7:13).

- His tears along with Mary's and the others' who were weeping over Lazarus's death illustrate that God understands our deepest pain (see John 11:35).
- The countercultural way He treated women and children demonstrates that God honors and values those who have been without honor and devalued. The first person He told that He was the Messiah was the woman at the well (see John 4:26).
- He was indignant when the disciples tried to keep children away from Him (see Mark 10:14). Little ones were important to Him, so important that He said the kingdom of heaven belongs to them (see Matthew 19:13-14), not to the snobby religious leaders who thought they deserved it.
- Jesus continually spoke to people's fears, demonstrating God's recognition that we are fearful people who need comfort (see Matthew 10:31; Mark 5:36; John 14:17). When the disciples thought Jesus was a ghost when He walked to meet them on the water, He immediately reassured them, "Take courage! It is I. Don't be afraid" (Matthew 14:27).
- Jesus healed the woman who for eighteen years was bent and crippled. When He took care of physical illnesses and weakness, He revealed that He knows that we are frail and weak and need His touch (see Luke 13:10-13).
- He knew fatigue and invites those who are weary to come to Him for rest (see Matthew 11:28).
- When He touched the leper, who had probably not had human touch for a long time (see Matthew 8:3), He demonstrated that He understands our need for human touch and gentleness.
- He understood that the spiritual issues surrounding Him were troubling. He showed His empathy when He said, "Do not let your hearts be troubled" (John 14:1).

To see Jesus is to see God. They are one and the same. Jesus showed us incredible love by taking our place and dying in our stead. Jesus' love and tenderness is God's.

Not only did God show His goodness to us through Jesus' life but He also communicates with us through Scripture.

We Can See His Goodness in His Written Word

Second Timothy 3:16 says, "All Scripture is God-breathed." God gave us His Word to guide us in how to live in this world. He didn't leave us to figure it out by ourselves.

Shelly:

Years ago Glen and I were at a crossroads. We were newly married and had good jobs, but we wanted more significant work, so we applied to several mission organizations and Christian ministries. The first acceptance letter surprised us. It had come so soon, and we weren't sure we were ready to go to live in another country. We decided to take a day off work to fast and pray for God's guidance. We agreed that we would each seek direction on our own and get back together at the end of the day to see what God had said to us.

As I sat in the bedroom of our tiny apartment, I found it hard to pray and read my Bible. What if God tells Glen to go and I get the message to stay? When I am looking to God for direction, I don't hunt around for a verse that "works." I ask God to speak to me from whatever passage I've been reading. Glen, I knew, was reading in a different part of the Bible. As I read, looked up cross-references, and prayed, I felt that God was telling me that we should go. Still I worried. Now that God has told me we should go, what do we do if He tells Glen to stay? As I prayed and read the rest of the day, I became more and more convinced that God was leading us to go. When Glen and I got together at the end of the day, I learned that

*God had given him the same direction and had even used some of the
same passages of Scripture to guide him! During the difficulties and
extreme challenges of the twenty years that we lived in Ecuador, we
repeatedly returned to that clear and specific direction that God had
given us through His Word.*

God's powerful Word directs our way. It gives us hope when there is
nothing to hope for; it tells us what our purpose is when we feel worth-
less. It is a sword to combat the Enemy's ferocious attacks. Not only
that, Scripture teaches us how to pray, how to communicate with God.
The truth in the Bible has the power to transform our lives. Through it
we learn that we can be radically free of our sin, shame, and guilt.

God's Word is good because it is "living and active. Sharper than
any double-edged sword, it penetrates even to dividing soul and spirit,
joints and marrow; it judges the thoughts and attitudes of the heart"
(Hebrews 4:12). Sometimes the written Word doesn't feel alive. Many
of us read our Bibles as if it were spam in our e-mail inbox. We're quick
to delete it because it does not seem to directly affect us. Contrast that
with reading love letters, where we carefully pore over each word for
meaning, relevance, and relationship. We don't read them once and
then throw them away; we read them over and over again, looking for
nuances of our loved one's love for us, savoring the tenderness.

The Bible is God's love letter to us. He woos us through all of
Scripture. As the two of us read God's Word, we intentionally look
for love calls to our hearts. For instance, in James 1:5 He promises to
give wisdom when we ask, "without finding fault"! If anyone has the
right to find fault with us, especially when we should have asked for
wisdom about the current circumstances a long time ago, it's God. But
He doesn't. Our experience is that the Lover of our souls meets our
individual needs. Passages that may not have spoken to us previously
come alive at our point of need. God wants His Word to fit our heart's
cry, to address the filters we use to view life.

So ask Him to show His love to you as you read. It may be difficult for you to believe that God would uniquely speak to you through His Word, but He wants to meet you there. When you understand this and approach the Bible as God's good, loving, and personal communication to you, it will penetrate your heart and begin to take root in your life.

When we believe that our good God wants a relationship with us, His Word comes alive. When we allow it to work in our hearts, the Holy Spirit in-spires — breathes into — the Word, giving it the power to transform us. First Thessalonians 2:13 paints the picture: "We also thank God continually because, when you received the word of God, which you heard from us, you accepted it not as the word of men, but as it actually is, the word of God, which is at work in you who believe."

God's Word has the power to speak directly to where we live, to address our questions and guide our actions. Years ago, Shelly saw God use His Word to speak specifically to a woman in her Spanish Bible study.

Shelly:

One morning before the study began, the women were talking and catching up on each other's lives. Maria's normally happy face was creased into worry lines as she grabbed my arm. With near desperation she said, "I've lied to my husband! During our prayer time will you pray about what I should do?" She went on to tell me that her Mercedes had been stolen from the parking lot of the mall where she was shopping. Upset, she had called the police, then her husband, insisting he come to pick her up. He told her that he was supposed to go to a critical meeting and that he might lose his job if he didn't attend. Still Maria begged him to come. He reluctantly agreed, warning her that he might not have a job by the end of the week. She didn't care. While her husband was on his way, she began to answer the policeman's questions and remembered that she had parked her car on the other side of the mall. It hadn't been stolen at all! When her husband arrived, Maria told him that the police had found the car. She said nothing to correct his idea that it had been stolen. Now she was afraid that her husband would be fired for missing the meeting. What would he do to her if he discovered the truth? I assured her we would bring her petition to the Father.

When the group settled down and began to share prayer requests, Maria couldn't contain herself. She repeated her need and began to cry. Her story riveted all of us. There was not a woman in the room who hadn't lied to her husband at one time or another, but never with such dire consequences!

When I could, I stopped the discussion and announced, "We're not going to tell Maria what to do; we are going to ask God to show her." I bowed my head and pleaded with the Lord to direct Maria, to heal her marriage, and to work His purposes in her and her husband's lives. When Maria found the passage we were studying, her eyes opened wide. She gasped and announced that she had to be the one to read it aloud.

The week before, we had ended in Ephesians 4, and now we were picking up at verse 25. Our Spanish translation started verse 25 with the words "Stop lying now!" The written Word of God pierced to the heart of Maria's issue. When the study was over, she told the group, "I've always wondered what Shelly means when she talks about hearing God's voice. Today I know. I am going to tell my husband the truth!"

Maria made good on what she had promised before God and the group. She lived out what James 1:22-25 says:

Do not merely listen to the word, and so deceive yourselves. Do what it says. Anyone who listens to the word but does not do what it says is like a [woman] who looks at [her] face in a mirror and, after

looking at [herself], goes away and immediately forgets what [she]
looks like. But the [woman] who looks intently into the perfect law
that gives freedom, and continues to do this, not forgetting what [she]
has heard, but doing it — [she] will be blessed in what [she] does.

Maria's "blessing" was that God used her honesty to increase the
joy and intimacy in her marriage and that her husband didn't lose his
job. When she responded to what God had shown her, she tasted His
goodness in new ways. Her marriage became stronger, the friendships
in the Bible study were solidified, and her faith, love, and closeness
with her Lord grew. Maria had experienced the living, active Word
cutting right to the heart of her situation. Her desire to know it more
became almost insatiable.

Jesus warned us that there will be trouble in this world (see John
16:33). He also said that the "cares and worries of this world," like
weeds, crowd out the Word in our hearts (see Matthew 13:22). But
God's Word will penetrate the soil of our hearts when, despite our
difficulties, we expect to hear from Him. When we listen for His voice,
God speaks.

When disappointment or heartache comes, we often respond as
Eve did. She lost sight of what she knew about God, but as we grow
in knowledge of our powerful God, we can strengthen our conviction
that He is good and that His ways and purposes for us are good. God
chose countless ways to show Himself to us. His fingerprints are all
over creation, revealing His character. As if that were not enough, He
sent His one and only Son, showing Himself to us in human form.
What a powerful demonstration of His deep desire for relationship
with us! God's Spirit continues to whisper His grand plan and purpose
through the written Word. The more we look, the more we see the
evidence of our Father's overwhelming goodness and love for us.

Gracious Father, we are awed at the design of the ages — that You reveal to us Your goodness through showing Yourself in creation, sending us Your Son, and giving us Your Word. When our hearts capture that truth in a small way, we can only say, "What we know has made us long to know You more." Holy One, tear away the calluses on our spirits until we respond to Your Word. We bow low in Your holy presence.

Holy Habits

- Verses to memorize: "You are good and kind and do good; teach me Your statutes. . . . I will keep Your precepts with my whole heart" (Psalm 119:68-69, AMP).

- Choose something good in creation that you see every day: a plant, a mountain, a tree. When you look at it, breathe the prayer *Show me Your goodness in the things You have made*. Become a student of the creation that God spoke into being. Let yourself revel in variations, intricacies, and new discoveries.

- Ask God to use creation to sensitize your heart and mind to His goodness. Sit quietly outside or take a walk by yourself. "Listen" to Him as you take note of the nature around you and thank Him for making it.

- Author Dallas Willard challenges people to read the Bible for "sweetness."[2] God promises, "With honey from the rock I would satisfy you" (Psalm 81:16). Choose a passage of Scripture (a short chapter or eight to ten verses) that you want to become a part of you. Read it daily for at least a week. Suck on a piece of hard candy each time you read. Deliberately savor the verses as you enjoy the candy. Slowly draw out the goodness and take it into yourself. Jeremiah enjoyed God's Word that way. He wrote, "When your words came, I ate them; they were my joy and my heart's delight, for I bear your name" (Jeremiah 15:16).

Here are some suggestions for passages to bask in: Psalm 139:1-6; 139:13-18; Romans 12:1-2; Ephesians 1:3-8; 3:14-21; Colossians 3:12-17; 2 Timothy 1:6-9; Hebrews 4:12-16; 1 Peter 1:3-9; 5:6-11; 2 Peter 1:3-8; 1 John 3:1-3.

- Whenever you open the Bible, pray, *Speak, Lord. Your servant is listening.* And let Him speak to you. Let His Word return to your heart in a fresh way and draw you ever deeper into a love relationship with Him.

- Prepare your heart before you go to church, a Bible study, a retreat, or a special meeting. Go expecting God to speak to you. For instance, you might use Fridays to start thinking about what God will say to you at church on Sunday. Ask Him to reveal to you anything that you need to make right with Him so that your heart is ready to hear what He has to say to you.

Responding to His Word

1. Read Psalm 19:1; 97:6; Acts 14:17; Romans 1:20. What do you discover about how God reveals Himself?
2. Mimi's friend's father never saw the Japanese emperor because he was hidden behind a curtain. Read Luke 23:45-46 and Hebrews 10:19-22. What do these passages tell us about the curtain separating God and man?
3. According to Hebrews 10:19-22, what do we have because of the open curtain?

4. Read John 1:1-3,14. Put yourself in John's shoes and write a paragraph about what it must have been like to see God's glory. How is that God's goodness?

5. Look at what Jesus did with God's Word in John 8:55. How can you follow His example?

6. Read James 1:22-25. What does it say about those who do not respond to the Word? What does it tell you to do?

7. Read Colossians 3:16. List some things you can do to realistically make this happen.

8. Read Ephesians 3:14-21 from the perspective that this is God's love letter to you. As you read, personalize the verses and put in your name wherever it says you or your. Does the passage speak to you in a different way? What did you learn from it?

9. Isaiah 55:10-11 describes some of the results of God's Word. What are they?

10. Read John 15:7. According to this verse, what will happen if we stay in the Word?

Chapter 3

Dancing in Life-Giving Light

The tropical air, mixed with the smell of salt and the rhythmic sound of the waves gently touching the beach just outside their window, helped Mimi and her husband feel relaxed and safe.

Mimi:

Cal and I were vacationing in the Galapagos Islands. The small town we were staying in turned off the power at midnight, plunging everything into darkness. The moonless night covered us under a blanket of quietness and tucked us in with a feeling of tranquility. We were sleeping deeply when suddenly I became aware of a touch. It took me a second to realize that Cal was sleeping on the other side of the bed and that what I felt had come from somewhere else in the darkness. I strained to hear something, but the lapping waves covered other sounds. Without light I could see nothing. Then I felt something brush my foot.

A shiver went up my body as I realized someone was in our room. Cal sat up as the door to our hotel room flew open. I barely discerned the silhouette of an intruder as he fled. We heard his feet pounding down the street, and then only the lapping waves. With racing hearts we groped for a flashlight. The brightness of the light revealed that the man had entered our room by cutting the window screen. He had crawled quietly over our luggage and stolen our money and other valuables.

The part that frightens me most when I think back over that night is how dark it was. I could not see. I have always had great vision, and up until that experience, I had relied on that gift. That night, I realized that we need more than good eyesight to see — we need light. My 20/20 vision is no good unless it is illuminated.

The Light Transforms the Darkness

We are so accustomed to physical light that we never consider what life would be like without it. The first verses of the Bible tell us that in the beginning, the earth was formless and empty and darkness covered its surface. Then God called for light. "God said, 'Let there be light,' and there was light. God saw that the light was good, and he separated the light from the darkness. God called the light 'day,' and the darkness he called 'night.' And there was evening, and there was morning — the first day" (Genesis 1:3-5). The fourth day, God created the sun and moon, and from that point on, from our human perspective, the sun became the "supreme metaphor of the glory of God."[1] God created the sun to pour its life-giving warmth over all the earth. We wake up to its light every day, regardless of whether we are good or evil.

Because of a longing to worship a higher being, many have looked no further than the sun in their search for God. Tribes perform dances in thanks for the sun's productivity but give no thought to its Creator. When we see God as the sun's Creator, we conclude that He is good because the sun provides light, warmth, growth, energy, seasons, and so much more. We could not survive without it.

Not only did God create physical light, He *is* light. During biblical times, people understood this. David declared, "The LORD is my light" (Psalm 27:1). Isaiah announced, "The LORD will be your everlasting light" (60:19). The apostle John told us that "God is light; in him there is no darkness at all" (1 John 1:5). When we open our lives to His salvation, we are inviting His light into us. Without Christ we are spiritually dead — in darkness. With Christ we are alive — dancing in the light.

God sent His light to the earth in the person of Jesus Christ, who said, "I am the light of the world. Whoever follows me will never walk in darkness, but will have the light of life" (John 8:12). One day as Jesus and His disciples were walking, they saw a man who had been born blind. They questioned the Master as to whether it was the man's or his parent's sin that was responsible for the man's blindness (see John 9:2-3). In those days, people believed that misfortune was punishment from God and blessings were rewards for good behavior. We hear similar teaching today.

That perspective creates a burden of darkness and unnecessary guilt when tragedy touches our lives. Jesus' life-giving answer was, "Neither this man nor his parents sinned. . . . This happened so that the work of God might be displayed in his life" (verse 3). What a relief to know that the man's blindness wasn't someone's fault. God's plan for the blind man, and for us, is that whatever darkness reaches our lives, He will use it for good. God wants to use the difficulties we face for His glory, and He will if we will allow Him to do that.

Immediately after Jesus' culturally upside-down explanation of the reason for the man's blindness, He announced to His disciples, "While I am in the world, I am the light of the world" (verse 5). Then He turned and told the blind man to go and wash in the Pool of Siloam. The Jews believed that the waters of this pool had special healing properties. Jesus didn't need to use the water to heal, but He sent the man to the pool to encourage his faith. He obeyed Jesus' instructions and went. When he returned, he could see. He had personally experienced Jesus as the light.

Eyesight and Heartsight

Jesus did not give the blind man a new pair of eyes; He simply opened the eyes he already had. Spiritually, we often look to God for something other than what we have rather than ask Him to infuse what we already have with the light of His Spirit. Instead of asking God to give us something new, we can ask Him to maximize what He has already provided. We can do this by praying, *Shine Your light in me so that I may see what You see. Use my eyes.* Our physical eyes cannot see without light. The light that illumines our physical and spiritual eyesight is a gift from the hand of our good God. Not only did God give us light, but He also gave us the eyes to see what that light illumines.

Even though our eyes enable us to see, we still need the Light of the World to understand what we see. We call this heartsight. Through Him we can become more aware of the physical world around us as well as the unseen spiritual realm. When we look at creation only through our human eyes and don't see the spiritual side, we lose the rich dimension of what God wants to illustrate. Our physical eyes can function but be sightless in the spiritual sense.

We see this in the reaction of the townspeople to the miracle. They were so blown away that they denied having known the healed man (see John 9:8-10). Even though he looked like the same person and went back home to the same house, wearing the same clothes, they could not believe that the one who was once blind could now see. The leaders of the church "hurled insults" at him, accused him of sin, and finally threw him out of the synagogue (see John 9:28-34). Who were the blind people at that point? Their reactions to the miracle remind us of the way we have seen some people respond to God's work today.

A friend recounted to us the time that doctors told her that her husband's heart was severely damaged after a heart attack. After she and their church body spent a weekend in intense prayer for healing, the physicians could not explain why they could no longer find any damage. Our friend told them that she believed God had healed her husband in answer to prayer. The doctors ignored her words. They were unwilling to accept that God might supernaturally intervene. The blind man's neighbors and church leaders also had to be willing to see and to acknowledge what God had done. "The light shines in the darkness, but the darkness has not understood it" (John 1:5). They had physical light and functioning eyes, but they did not see or understand the spiritual dimension in the healing that took place. They had eyesight but not heartsight. Saddest of all, they missed knowing the Light of the World! When we look for God's light and acknowledge it, we will see His work.

Our friend Ann is a talented musician. When she plays the piano, everyone she accompanies sounds better than they really are. Ann has played since she was a young girl, but when she was in her mid-sixties, she began having trouble with her left hand. At first it felt heavy and wouldn't cooperate, and then soon she was unable to open it. It wasn't long before her hand was completely shriveled and hung limply at her side. Doctors told her that they could do nothing. She would never be able to play the piano again. We wondered how Ann was dealing with the death of her lifelong identity as a musician.

The next time we saw her, her once beautiful fingers were curled into a permanent fist, yet she was radiant, even more beautiful than we remembered. She told us that as she watched her hand shrivel and close, God began to give her a new perspective on her situation. Ann told us that as it became increasingly obvious that her piano-playing days were over, she grieved, wondering, *Who am I now that I can't play the piano?* She said that God began to show her an identity in Him that she had never known before. Her joy came from truly seeing who she was because of Christ, not because of what she did. With His help, she had gained heartsight.

Paul wanted the Ephesian believers to receive heartsight when he said, "I pray . . . that the eyes of your heart may be enlightened"

(Ephesians 1:18). Because Ann learned to dance in the light with her Lord, His light illumined the eyes of her heart. As she understood His point of view, she came to terms with her loss of skill and identity. Ann's glow was the result of finding her significance and seeing her situation through the filter of God's abundant goodness.

We need God to open the eyes of our understanding, just as we need Him to breathe into our bodies to give us life. The psalmist said, "In your light we see light" (Psalm 36:9). He understood the need to hold up the lamp of God's truth in our world. Because light is part of God's eternal character, His light is always available to us for spiritual understanding.

When the light of God initially touches a heart, a person's spiritual eyesight is weak and things appear to be "formless and empty" (Genesis 1:2), like the condition of the earth before God created light. We see this illustrated in the story of the formerly blind man. When he sees physical light for the first time and by it is able to see the things and people around him, he does not recognize Jesus as the man who healed him. He simply says that he has heard that He is a "man they call Jesus" (John 9:11). The blind man's understanding was blurry, shallow, and general. Then, as his understanding increases, he declares that Jesus "is a prophet" (verse 17). Finally, as the light of Christ goes to the core of his heart, he declares, "Lord, I believe" (verse 38), and he worships. Not only did Jesus give this man eyesight, He gave him heartsight as well. He opened the eyes of his spiritual understanding. The light of God can do the same in our lives.

When the Light of the World hung on the cross, darkness fell over all the land (see Matthew 27:45). The blackness represented God's grief over sin, the state of the human heart, and that He could not look on it. A wonderful passage in Isaiah that promises the coming of Jesus says that "the people walking in darkness have seen a great light; on those living in the land of the shadow of death a light has dawned" (9:2). Jesus came to take away darkness, but we have to allow Him to remove our individual spiritual darkness, just as the blind man in John 9 allowed Him to remove his physical blindness.

The Indwelling Light

One day when Mimi was shopping in a bazaar in Cairo, Egypt, going in and out of dark, dingy stores hunting for treasures, she found some beautiful handblown, multicolored glass balls.

Mimi:

It was sheer pleasure for me to select a collection for those I loved. However, it wasn't until I saw the glass ornaments in daylight that I actually saw how truly exquisite they were. Sunshine caught the glass and made the colors and designs shimmer and dance. This has become a metaphor for me about what happens when we invite Christ into our lives. He puts His light into the darkness of our souls. We then become Light catchers.

There is something so transforming about stepping into the light of God's presence that we *become* light. Jesus said to believers, "You are the light of the world" (Matthew 5:14). Jesus also declared, "I am the light of the world" (John 9:5), as well as, "I am the way and the truth and the life" (John 14:6). He never said that *we* are the way, truth, or life. Jesus made several "I am" statements,[2] but the only one that we share with Him is that we are also light: "God, who said, 'Let light shine out of darkness,' made his light shine in our hearts to give us the light of the knowledge of the glory of God in the face of Christ. But we have this treasure in jars of clay to show that this all-surpassing power is from God and not from us" (2 Corinthians 4:6-7). When God's light is in us, it shines forth.

Did you ever notice that when you light a candle in a pot, the light is much more visible if the pot is full of holes? That's what we are. We are cracked pots: broken people in whom God has chosen to place His light. We have no light of our own. Our goodness comes from His goodness. When we invite Him to put His Spirit inside us, we don't have to generate His light; we just house the light God gives us.

Walking in the Light

We can step into God's light, take His hand, and walk in the light. Walking in the light is choosing to live in the light He has given us. When we do, we grow to know Him ever more deeply and He will give us even more light.

When God said, "Let there be light," He created an analogy of Himself. Light is a physical representation of who His is; it is a foundational aspect of His character. When we walk in the light, God pours His character through us. However, it involves *our* choice. It is not enough to simply want to be in God's light. We must give our mind, body, soul, and spirit over to Him, allowing His character to be formed in us. When we do that, we put ourselves in His light and can choose to stay there.

Think of it this way. Imagine that you are an actor on a stage with a spotlight. You can choose to move out of the spotlight, or you can choose to stay in it. God's light is the spotlight, but we must place ourselves in it. Following Jesus Christ is walking in the light. When we obey Him, we are in His light.

Walking in the light has several benefits:

Light points the way to Christ. "Those who are wise will shine like the brightness of the heavens, and those who lead many to righteousness, like the stars for ever and ever" (Daniel 12:3).

You may wonder how you can make an impact, just one small person in a dark place. *I'm one believer. What difference can I make here?* You can just be God's light wherever you are, whatever you do.

Mimi:

Cal and I had just returned to the Middle East after an extended time away, and I was looking forward to reacquainting myself with the neighborhood merchants. One morning I walked into a vegetable shop, and the owner turned to me and said, "Has the light returned to my store?" I was delighted that he had seen God's light in me. Even though I could not speak to this man about Jesus, I prayed that God's light would point the way for him to know it himself.

Never forget this truth: Darkness cannot absorb light. Even though we may feel insignificant and unimportant in our humanness, God's light can shine through us.

Shelly:

When we first returned to the States to live, I felt as though I had been dropped down a long tunnel. I was going through culture shock, and everything looked and felt different. But I was sure that God was good, He was with us, and I could stand on His faithfulness.

I was asked to teach a women's Bible study at our church. One of my acquaintances brought some of her friends to the study. One of them, Liliana, had touched a Bible only a few times in her life, and when someone gave her one to follow along in, she held it gingerly, as if she were afraid. She sat next to one of the church grandmas, who helped her find the verses I cited. Liliana's eyes shimmered with tears.

After the second class, she insisted that we talk privately. As the two of us sat in a doorway, sweating in the hot Florida sun, she broke down. "I have to have what you have!" Confused about what she meant, I mentally reviewed what I had at the time: loneliness, isolation, bewilderment, discouragement, even fear. How could she possibly want any of these things? Then I realized what she had seen in me: Jesus! The light of His goodness in me had spoken to her so

deeply that she couldn't see the scared little girl inside of me. I gently
explained to her that what she saw in me was Jesus and that she
could have Him too.

Even though you may not be a missionary or Bible teacher, if you have received Jesus, you too are a "Light catcher." Because you are one of a kind, created by God, your life will uniquely show Jesus. With His light in you, you can show His goodness to those around you.

Our friend Barbi (whom you met in chapter 1) hungers to know God deeply. One way she uniquely reflects Jesus is that she draws people into her ever-deepening intimacy with God. Years ago she started an annual getaway for her friends with the sole purpose of growing with God and each other. We wish you could be at one of those retreats. Barbi orchestrates things so that the happy laughter, deep conversations, tears, times of worship, prayer, teaching, and quiet, combined with adventuring, all join together to help women discover God in a whole-life experience. Barbi dances in the light of Christ and, because of that, uniquely shines it on others.

Stephany, another friend, loves to bake. She is always trying new dessert recipes. Each family member enjoys a piece and the rest goes into the freezer. One day as she was trying to cram another baked treat into her bulging freezer, Stephany wondered if there was a way she could share the bounty. She called the local rescue mission to find out if they could use desserts. The hearty "yes" prompted her to take all the baked goods she had and share them with homeless men and women, many who had forgotten what a home-cooked goodie tasted like. Stephany uniquely shines Jesus' light each week as she and her daughters deliver homemade treats to the rescue mission.

We probably couldn't do what Barbi and Stephany do, and likely you couldn't either. That's okay. You weren't meant to. God made you to be you, a Light catcher uniquely formed by Him — unlike any other — to shimmer and sparkle as you bask in Him.

Light convicts of sin. "He will bring to light what is hidden in darkness and will expose the motives of men's hearts" (1 Corinthians 4:5). The Light of God brings with it conviction of sin. We are not responsible to convict others.

Shelly:

As I talked to Liliana about acknowledging her sin, I quickly realized she didn't believe she had committed any. So, trusting that God would take care of the sin issues, I explained to her how to put Him in charge, making Him Lord of her life. After she invited Jesus to be Lord of her life, her attitude about sin began to change. It was not long before she began to talk about confessing her wrongdoings.

Famous preacher and author Bishop Fulton J. Sheen says,

The closer a person approaches God, the less worthy he feels. A painting under candlelight shows fewer defects than under the brilliance of the sun; so too the souls who are some distance from God feel more certain of their moral integrity than those who are very close to Him. Those who have left the lights and glamour of the world, and for years have been irradiated by His countenance, have been the foremost to acknowledge themselves as freighted down with the great burden of sin.[3]

Light generates fellowship with other believers. "If we walk in the light, as he is in the light, we have fellowship with one another" (1 John 1:7). Our friend Connie told us about the day she flew to her father's funeral. Two weeks earlier, her husband of eighteen years had died from stomach cancer. She was worn out from grieving and from the weight of caring for him during his last days, making funeral arrangements, and visiting with many family members and visitors. During her first night sleeping in her emptier-than-ever house, Connie's sister called to tell her that their father had died suddenly.

She flung things into a suitcase and rushed to the airport. On the way, she called her employer to arrange for more compassionate leave; she'd been back to work only a week since her husband's funeral. Her boss said, "Connie, we can't afford to give you more time. If you go, don't bother coming back." Stunned, she managed to get herself onto the plane, asking God for help. She was distressed to see that her seat was between two others way in the back of the packed jetliner. When she collapsed into her chair, she buried her face in her hands. The woman in the aisle seat put a warm hand on her shoulder and wordlessly comforted her. Connie began to cry. "I know all things work together for good, but it doesn't look like it right now," she said. Her seatmate said, "I believe that too. It seems like your heart is very heavy. Do you want to talk about it?"

Connie poured her story out to the woman, who she came to think of as an angel of light. They cried together, and her seatmate comforted her with Scripture. By the time the plane landed, they had cried, laughed, and shared secrets like best friends. Connie said, "Because we both knew Jesus, we enjoyed sweet fellowship. God answered my prayer for help."

Light gives direction and guidance. "Send forth your light and your truth, let them guide me; let them bring me to your holy mountain, to the place where you dwell" (Psalm 43:3).

We often think that we should ask God for only "big" things — whether to move or take a job, whom to marry, where to go to church, how to guide our wayward child. But God guides us in *everything*, and we can look to Him for direction in simple decisions as well as the large challenges of our lives.

Mimi:

I once told some women that I even ask God which fruit to choose in the grocery store. They were shocked that I would "bother" God with such a simple detail. My response was, "Well, if Eve had consulted God about the fruit, we might not be in the mess we're in now!"

God's light gives us direction and leads His children, even when we're only asking about which kind of apples to buy. Pillars of clouds by day and fire by night represented the Light of His presence for the Israelites. Today He guides us with His Spirit: "When he, the Spirit of truth, comes, he will guide you into all truth" (John 16:13).

Light gives understanding. "In your light we see light" (Psalm 36:9). Before we received Him, the Spirit of God was waiting, hovering over our lives to bring order, harmony, and beauty. Even before He gave us light and made us a light, He provided enough light for the path so we could find Him. "The light on the inside will guide you, a reasoning soul, to understand the facts revealed by common days and nights you cannot understand otherwise."[4] Because His Light is in us, we can see and understand things beyond us. This is a reality for us in a way that most Old Testament saints never imagined. The Holy Spirit sent by God works in us. We are truly enlightened.

Shelly:

One morning years ago, God enlightened my understanding of 1 Peter 3:1, "Wives, in the same way be submissive to your husbands." I did not like the idea of submitting to my husband and could never understand why God had put this verse in the Bible. One of my holy habits is to ask God to give light to the Scriptures, and that's what I did that morning even though I was pretty sure I wouldn't like the answer. I had probably read the verse hundreds of times, but I saw four words I had never noticed before: "in the same way." I wondered, What does that phrase refer to?

I picked up the thread in 1 Peter 2:21, "To this you were called, because Christ suffered for you, leaving you an example, that you should follow in his steps." The passage goes on to say, "Instead, he entrusted himself to him who judges justly" (verse 23) and "the Shepherd and Overseer of your souls" (verse 25). God's light helped clarify what "in the same way" is referring to. I saw that submission

*is about following Christ's example. It became instantly clear that
when I submit to my husband, I can entrust myself to Him who
judges justly, the One who is the Shepherd and Overseer of my soul,
knowing that He is greater than any human authority in my life.
It made me see that just as Jesus looked beyond his human circumstances to His Father, I can submit to Glen for God's sake! His light
penetrated the bewilderment that those verses held for me.*

The Light helps us love others. "Whoever loves his brother lives
in the light" (1 John 2:10). Our friend Adela's only son was in his early
twenties when he was brutally attacked and murdered by a young man
attempting to steal the family car. The murderer's cruelty and lack of
remorse horrified us all. The pictures of the crime scene in the newspa-
per gave us nightmares. We wondered how Adela would hold up under
the heavy grief. Several months after the murder, before the case went to
trial, Adela went and visited her son's murderer in jail. She looked him
in the eyes and said, "I am a follower of Jesus Christ, and I came here to
tell you that I forgive you for killing my son. I pray for you every day."

When Adela told us the story, she said, "My son's murderer looked
at me but never responded. Since then, I've asked to see him multiple
times and he refuses. The only other time I've seen him was at the trial.
God has given me love and compassion for that confused, wounded
young man. I still pray for him daily." Adela had every human reason
to hate the man who killed her son, but she walks in God's light. It is
God in her that allows her to love the unlovable.

The Dark Night of the Soul

You may be reading this thinking, *I've tried to walk in the light and
follow Jesus. I'm trying to obey Him, but all I feel is darkness.* You are
not alone. We have both felt that way. In fact, nearly everyone we know
who has a deep relationship with God has gone through periods of

personal darkness. Even Mother Teresa struggled with it during much of her life.

The concept of the "dark night of the soul" came from the writings of Saint John of the Cross, who lived in the sixteenth century. It is described this way:

> *In the* Christian *tradition, one who has developed a strong* prayer *life and consistent devotion to* God *suddenly finds traditional prayer extremely difficult and unrewarding for an extended period of time during this "dark night." The individual may feel as though God has suddenly abandoned them or that his or her prayer life has collapsed. . . . Rather than resulting in devastation, however, the dark night is perceived . . . to be a blessing in disguise.*[5]

Shelly:

I've experienced this dark night of the soul. During this period, it felt as if my prayers bounced off the ceiling. I couldn't feel God's presence. It was as though my dearest friend had died. I checked my heart for sin and confessed anything that I could possibly think of. Nothing worked. As days dragged into months and months into years, I kept on doing what I knew was right: reading my Bible, confessing sin, trying to pray, being with others who loved God, going to church. The phrase that our youth pastor pounded into us when we were in high school was the theme of my life: "Never doubt in the darkness what God has shown you in the light." Nothing made a difference.

Slowly, pinpricks of light penetrated the heavy fog. After my own dark night, I read a verse that, for a long time, had been only words on a page. God says in Isaiah 45:3, "I will give you the treasures of darkness, riches stored in secret places, so that you may know that I am the LORD, the God of Israel, who summons you by name." At the time, I found no treasures in my darkness, nothing was rich.

However, as I look back on the long period of heaviness, I see that the riches and treasures that came from it are invaluable. Everything about who God is became so real because I hadn't felt His presence for so long. I came to know God's goodness, love, and commitment to me in new ways. I recognize that even in my personal darkness, God was there, and through it I came to enjoy His light more than I could imagine. I have learned to dance in it. I wouldn't trade that experience for anything.

Being Light in a Dark World

The world around us is full of darkness, and it could overwhelm us. However, we have learned that the more we walk in the light of God's goodness, the more light He gives us. "We, who with unveiled faces all reflect the Lord's glory [light], are being transformed into his likeness with *ever-increasing* glory, which comes from the Lord, who is the Spirit" (2 Corinthians 3:18, emphasis added). Many times we aren't even aware of the ever-increasing light that is a part of who we are when we grow to know Him more. We'll close this chapter by telling you a story that illustrates this point.

One Halloween, Sally called a friend of hers from her hospital room. She was frightened because her roommate was involved in witchcraft. Sally knew the dangers of the occult and the increased activity of evil on the last night of October. She was especially afraid of her roommate that night. Together she and her friend recounted how the God of Israel neither slumbers nor sleeps, how His blood was shed to win victory over darkness, and how her heavenly Father would watch over her. They prayed together on the phone.

Before Sally went to bed that night, she prayed again. She was sure that God was stronger than Satan and his forces. When she woke the next morning, her roommate announced, "Did you know that a light surrounds your bed?" Sally realized that although she had turned off her bedside lamp, God had covered her in His light while she slept. She gained a new sense of security and belonging because of God's protection over her that night.

God's light is life-giving. When we walk in His light, it frees us to dance through our nights, our days, and into our future, absolutely confident in His goodness.

Good God of Light, open our eyes to see more of You. May we be ever more open to the convicting work of Your light. May we pierce the darkness of this world with Your light in us. Thank You for the privilege of carrying the treasure of who You are — good light — within the earthen vessels that we are. We love You.

Holy Habits

- Verses to memorize: "They feast on the abundance of your house; you give them drink from your river of delights. For with you is the fountain of life; in your light we see light" (Psalm 36:8-9).

- Each morning when you reach to switch on the light by your bed or in the bathroom, stop for a moment. Thank God for the light He gives you spiritually and physically. Ask Him to remind you of the light He has already given you, and then walk in that light.

- Light a candle as you read your Bible. Use it as a reminder that His light guides you as you read His Word.

- Find something that catches the light: a glass, shiny piece of metal, prism, or something else. Put it someplace that catches the sun. When you look at it, remind yourself that you are to be a Light catcher, a reflection of Him.

- Think of someone who is hard for you to love. Every day (for at least a week) ask God to bless that person. Be specific about how you want Him to bless. Pray that He will give you His perspective — heartsight — into that difficult person and teach you how to love him or her.

Responding to His Word

1. Jesus said, "I am the light of the world. Whoever follows me will never walk in darkness, but will have the light of life" (John 8:12). He also tells believers, "You are the light of the world" (Matthew 5:14). What do you think it means that He makes us light? How can you let His light shine in you?

2. Read Romans 1:21. Why does Paul say that their "foolish hearts were darkened"? Make a note of ways you can keep your heart from being darkened.

3. Make a list of at least ten things you are deeply thankful for. Spend some time thanking God for those things.

4. Read Ephesians 1:6,12,14. What is the parallel between the recurring phrase there and God's plan for the blind man in John 9?

5. What if Jesus had not healed the blind man? (He did not heal everyone. At the Pool of Bethesda, only one was healed [see John 5:2-8].) Would His purposes still have been accomplished? How much would that have depended on the blind man? Think about the challenges in your life. If God chooses not to remove them, how can you choose to live "to the praise of His glory" (Ephesians 1:14, NASB)?

6. In John 9:39, Jesus gives the spiritual reason for His coming to the world. Share an example of those "who see will become blind" in our society today. Think of an example from your own life of how God's light opened up your spiritually blind eyes, giving you heartsight.

7. Read Ephesians 1:18-21. Paul prayed that the eyes of our hearts be enlightened so that we may know what? How could knowing those things impact your life?

8. When we pray for people who don't know God, we often ask Him to show Himself to them. Is that a sound request according to Scripture? How might the example of Ephesians 1:18-20 affect your prayer for someone who doesn't believe?

9. Using the principles you discovered in question 8, write out a prayer for someone you know who has not yet received Christ. Express to God what you long to have happen to the person's spiritual condition.

10. First Peter 2:9 states God's purpose for having "called you out of darkness into his wonderful light." What is His purpose? The passage also lists four things He has made us, now that we are in His light. What are they? Ask God how you can live up to His design for you.

Chapter 4

Swept Off Your Feet

Shelly will never forget the day she realized that God loved *her*.

Shelly:

It was Valentine's Day and my little sister had received a valentine from her boyfriend, the best-looking guy in our church. He was my age, and I thought that he should have been my boyfriend. It didn't help that he had a driver's license and a pilot's license or that my sister was living a jet-set life.

In tears I ran into my bedroom. Would anyone ever love me? Was I so undesirable, so unlovable? *My mom knew I was upset and tiptoed into my room to talk. "Since today is the day that everybody celebrates love," she said, "why don't you do a word study on love in your Bible?" Frankly, I didn't want to hear that advice. But Mom was right. After she left, I rolled over, grabbed my Bible, turned to the concordance, and began looking up verses.*

I read that:

- *God is abounding in love. (see Exodus 34:6)*
- *His love endures forever. (see 2 Chronicles 5:13)*

- *His love is unfailing. (see Psalm 31:10 and many other places)*

The reality of what I was reading began to soothe the ache in my heart. When I read, "He crowns me with love and compassion" (see Psalm 103:4), I held my head up a little straighter. After all, who would not want someone to adorn her with love and compassion?

As I read Song of Solomon 2:4, "His banner over me is love," I thought, Who needs a Valentine's Day card? *I pictured myself walking around with a huge sign over my head, written by God Himself, stating, "I LOVE YOU, SHELLY!" Daniel 9:4 told me what kind of promise stands behind that banner: "[He] keeps his covenant of love with all who love him." I knew that a covenant is an unbreakable promise, especially when God makes it. Then in 1 John 3:1, I read that He lavishes His love on me!*

Romans 8 promises,

Who shall separate us from the love of Christ? Shall trouble or hardship or persecution or famine or nakedness or danger or sword? . . . No, in all these things we are more than conquerors through him who loved us. For I am convinced that neither death nor life, neither angels nor demons, neither the present nor the future, nor any powers, neither height nor depth, nor anything else in all creation, will be able to separate us from the love of God that is in Christ Jesus our Lord. (verses 35,37-39)

As I read, I knew I had found a life-changing truth: I can depend on God's love, and nothing can separate me from it. His love for me is far greater and far deeper than what I could imagine.

God swept me off my feet that day. I finally understood what it meant that the King of kings and Lord of lords had been wooing me all my life. My parents say that from then on everything about me changed. The way I dressed, walked, and talked was different, because I wanted to please the One on whose love I could depend. While the cute guy who liked my sister did not hang around, the Lord's love for me grows sweeter and sweeter, even after all these years.

The Sweetest Love

Some of you may identify with Shelly's story, but many people don't. Some gain an instant understanding of His love when they first encounter Christ, but for others, experiencing God's love is a foreign concept. Even though it might not be part of your experience, His love is a significant part of what it means that God is good. Coming to know His love is a supernatural thing that He makes available to all of us. For some it happens at an early age; for others it happens later. But it's never too late to be swept off your feet by His astonishing love.

It begins when you let yourself be "wooable," when you want and wait for Him to call you to Himself in a new way. Ask Him to help you fall in love with Him. Read His Word and personalize it. Read it realizing that He is speaking directly to you. Look for His love calls.

That's what Nina did. She has walked with God for many years and has led hundreds of people to Christ. But when some friends noticed there was something different about her, she said, "Every morning before I read my Bible, it has become my habit to simply sit and 'let' God love me. It's made such a difference. I have known Him for a long time, but I never felt His love for me this way. I have to choose to take the time and allow it to happen."

Teresa also grew up in the church; every time its doors opened, her family was there. She knew the Bible stories, how to behave like a good churchgoer, and the difference between right and wrong. When she was in college, she began using drugs, drinking alcohol, and being sexually promiscuous. All the while, she kept going to church. She continued living that way until finally, in midlife, amid great personal emptiness, she cried out to God and experienced, for the first time, His personal love for her. Today, Teresa is a radiant, transformed woman. When life pushed her to the limit, she let go of her traditional relationship with God (church attendance and saying the right things). In her desperation, she let her defenses down and was captivated by God's passionate love for her.

There is a hole inside each of us that only God can fill. Even a husband or closest friend can't meet all our needs like God can. If we expect them to, we will be disappointed. God's love is the sweetest any of us can ever experience. He will always have our best interest in mind. We are never far from His thoughts.

God's good love is:

Eternal. The psalmist declared, "May your unfailing love rest upon us, O LORD, even as we put our hope in you" (Psalm 33:22). Isn't it wonderful that we can never "use up" God's love? It will last forever, and nothing can separate us from it. No human love is like that. When Jesus went back to heaven, God's love continued. Hebrews 7:25 tells us that "he always lives to intercede" for us.

Self-existent. God doesn't need us; He *wants* us. 1 John 4:19 declares, "We love because he first loved us." Human love is born out of need, but God does not need our love. It does not complete Him. He is whole without us. Because He does not need us, God's self-existent love is always for our good.

Abundant. "The grace of our Lord was more than abundant, with the faith and love which are found in Christ Jesus" (1 Timothy 1:14, NASB). The idea of abundance is that it will never run out. It is not stingy or miserly. God doesn't just love you enough; He loves you abundantly!

Mimi:

When I think of God's love, I think of the pool dug in the floor of the Ituri Forest, which was our family's water supply. My brother, sister, and I loved walking down the jungle path near our home to the cool, shaded place where my father had built the pool. We were always alert in case wild animals were using the same spot to quench their thirst.

The tiny opening in the bottom of the pool held a particular fascination for me. Underground water bubbled out continually, never changing. People told us that it had been that way for years and that the same amount of water flowed from the spring, even when no one was watching.

We were thankful for our water supply, but we couldn't show gratitude to the spring. Day after day, year after year, we simply took from it as the spring continued to provide water. It kept giving because deep within the earth there was plenty more water. God's abundant love is like that. God is sometimes referred to as the "fountainhead of love." Our jungle water supply is a picture of God's deep spring of endless love.

Holy. His love is pure and complete — whole. "We know and rely on the love God has for us. God is love. Whoever lives in love lives in God, and God in him. In this way, love is made complete among us" (1 John 4:16-17). Holy love from our good, holy God is never dirty or sordid, never selfish or egotistical.

All-wise. "Oh, the depth of the riches of the wisdom and knowledge of God! How unsearchable his judgments, and his paths beyond tracing out!" (Romans 11:33). Because God's love is wise, you can trust Him. He will never give you too much or too little. He will not keep anything good from those who walk with Him (see Psalm 84:11).

Transcendent. God's love covers humanity, now and forever. "The earth is full of his unfailing love" (Psalm 33:5). The transcendence of God's love means that He sees the big picture of our lives, beginning to end. He is over it all. He lovingly and transcendently deals with us in our daily lives while keeping the full outlook of our lives under His loving care.

Omnipotent. "The weakness of God is stronger than man's

strength" (1 Corinthians 1:25). His power stands behind every facet of His love for us. There is nothing weak about that love. It is God's tenderness, executed with the strong arm of His power.

Unconditional. "He is kind [even] to the ungrateful and wicked" (Luke 6:35). The treasure of His unconditional love is that we cannot earn it or buy it. There is nothing we can do that will make Him love us any more or any less than He already does. He freely offers His love with no requirements to all who will receive it.

Selfless. "You know the grace of our Lord Jesus Christ, that though he was rich, yet for your sakes he became poor, so that you through his poverty might become rich" (2 Corinthians 8:9). Jesus did not consider "equality with God something to be grasped, but made himself nothing, taking the very nature of a servant, being made in human likeness" (Philippians 2:6-7). God came to earth, descending into what some translations say were "the lower earthly regions," putting aside His royalty. He who had never sinned became sin and went to the cross for us. "[It] would not be the surrender to death but the laying bare the heart of God's love. The love of God was made visible in sacrifice. On Calvary, He would prove Himself man by dying as every other man dies but He would prove Himself Divine by dying as no other man dies."[1]

Generous. "For God so loved . . . he gave his one and only Son, that whoever believes in him shall not perish but have eternal life" (John 3:16). God's love is so generous it extends to the entire world. In other words, it "includes every man, of every kind in every age."[2] How amazing to think that the outstretched arms of Jesus, as He hung on the cross, were open to all while at the same time they are open to each one of us as individuals. When you step into His arms, they close around you and you become His very own, held in the "everlasting arms" (Deuteronomy 33:27).

Always-offered. God is the father in the story of the prodigal son. He waits daily for His child to come home, and when He finally sees him on the horizon, He hitches up His clothes and takes off running to receive His son, arms wide open, heart full of love. God does the same for you. He eagerly waits to enfold you in His arms.

Joyfully-given. Zephaniah 3:17 tells us that God takes great joy in us: "He will take great delight in you, he will quiet you with his love, he will rejoice over you with singing." One of the ways that God delights in you and expresses His love for you is in song. It's not just any song. Imagine the exquisite beauty of the sound when the very Creator of music sings over you. Every other piece of music is a feeble reflection. God sings over you and is committed to you. Solomon said in 2 Chronicles 6:14, "O LORD, God of Israel, there is no God like you in heaven or on earth — you who keep your covenant of love with your servants."

God's love continues to cause lifeless souls to be filled with the joy of being wanted. He created and redeemed us for intimacy and wants to meet all our longings for deep relationship.

As A. W. Tozer points out,

> It is of the nature of love that it cannot lie quiescent. It is active, creative. . . . The love of God is one of the great realities of the universe, a pillar upon which the hope of the world rests. But it is a personal, intimate thing, too. God does not love populations, He loves people. He loves not masses, but men. He loves us all with a mighty love that has no beginning and can have no end.[3]

When we are aware of this, we will live loved. We will live in the circle of His goodness.

Nothing to Take for Granted

It's easy for those of us who have grown up in the church or been Christians for a long time to grow casual about God's love, to take it for granted. It must have been the same for the New Testament church. Perhaps that is why Paul wrote this prayer for the Ephesians: "I pray that you, being rooted and established in love, may have power, together with all the saints, to grasp how wide and long and high and deep is the love of Christ, and to know this love that surpasses knowledge" (Ephesians 3:17-19).

What is the width, length, height, and depth of God's love? Some see the physical cross as a symbol of it. Its shape expresses the extent of God's love for us. The top of the cross points toward heaven, the bottom points toward the earth, while the crossing arms indicate the far horizons. God's demonstrated His love for us at great cost, as the following chart shows:

What Jesus Had as Son of God	What Jesus Got as Son of Man
He was in the heart of the eternal Father	He was held to the heart of an earthly mother
He was the Son of God	He became the Son of Man
He was the Infinite	He became an infant
He held the world in His arms	His mother's arms held Him
His garment was space	He was wrapped in cloths
His home was heaven	He came to a stable and had no place to lay His head
He made the universe	He labored at a workbench
He wore royal garments	He wore peasant clothes and a bloodstained robe
He was sovereign	He endured jeers and mocking
He sat on a heavenly throne	He hung on the cross
He was without sin	He became sin for us
He was the Father's delight	He became the God-forsaken
He lit the stars	He lay in dust

Jesus came, He worked, He hungered and thirsted, He wept, suffered, bled, and because of love, He died.[4]

God showed His profound love for us by sending Jesus to redeem us and make relationship with Him possible. We can know that intellectually, even accept His love, yet not feel the depth of His love, especially when things aren't going the way we think they should.

Shelly:

Even though I personally had felt God's love for me in my teen years, there have been periods of time when my circumstances seemed to be saying that God didn't care about me anymore. This was particularly true during the years Glen and I struggled with infertility. During that time, the visits to the doctor, medications, and procedures took their toll on my emotions. I sometimes felt that God was playing with me, filling me with hope after one doctor's visit and then throwing me into despair with conflicting diagnoses from others. I struggled to rejoice with those who rejoiced, especially the year when it seemed as though all my friends were having babies but I wasn't. My heart ached. Before I had always been able to look to God's love to meet my needs, but His seeming unwillingness to give me what I longed for threw me into bewilderment.

Glen and I looked into adoption, and after a short while we learned about a young woman in Oregon who was willing to arrange a private adoption for her unborn child. We waited for news of the birth with bated breath. A month before the baby was due, I was at a conference on Ecuador's coast, which was nine hours away by car. During that conference, after much struggle and agony, I came to the place where I said to God, "I give my hopes and dreams to You. If You don't have children in our future, I will rest in Your love."

At that same time, a political problem boiled to the surface and the entire province went on strike. Strikes in Ecuador often include blocking roads with burning tires and nail strips, stopping all traffic.

Gangs man the roadblocks, threatening violence to anyone who dares try to run the blockades. I was stuck behind strike lines and didn't know when I would be able to return home. I walked several miles along a bumpy dirt road from the camp to the closest town and stood in line for a phone so that I could leave a message at Glen's office to let him know I was not going to be back as scheduled.

When Glen returned to his office, there were two messages awaiting him. One was from me and the other was a notice that a telegram had arrived. The telegram read, "COULDN'T WAIT. CAME EARLY. WAITING FOR MOMMY AND DADDY TO COME GET ME. WEIGHED 6 LBS, 9 OZS, 20 IN. LONG. LOVE YOU. WILLIAM CARL." My parents had been given temporary custody of the baby and had sent the telegram in his name.

What followed was a blur — thirty-six hours of miracles, a Hollywood-style rescue from behind strike lines, getting things in order to leave, throwing clothes into suitcases, and arranging plane tickets, exit papers, and other things that normally were impossible to accomplish in such a short time.

After long hours of travel, Glen and I finally stepped off the plane in Oregon. We didn't expect to see our son until we arrived at where he was staying. However, we were thrilled to see my father, along with my sister and her husband, who had flown in to surprise us. My dad gently led us over to a quiet section of the airport and out from behind a pillar stepped my mother with Carl, who was five days old. Glen and I were both crying. When the little bundle was placed in my arms, it was as if his tiny hand reached up and grabbed my heart forever.

Even though Carl was colicky and screamed in pain, everything about mothering gave me great pleasure, even the dirty diapers. I was up many times a night, sometimes for hours, trying to calm him. One night Carl had been up screaming, but his misery eased and he finally fell asleep. I was rocking him, reluctant to let go of the sweet moment. As I looked at his little face, I thought about the love that I had for Carl and how it was unlike anything I had experienced before. It had taken me over, occupied me. It got me out of bed when I was exhausted.

I looked down at our son and thought, I love you so much I would give my life for you. *And I heard (not audibly, but powerfully) God say, "That's what I did for you." "Yes, I know that God," I replied. "And if you love me as much as I love Carl, I'm awed, overjoyed, amazed. Thank You." A new awareness of God's love washed over me. Could He possibly love me more than I loved our little boy? It seemed impossible. We continued our conversation. "Shelly, your love for Carl is human. You will not always be there for him. You will get tired and fail, and your love is imperfect. But you can depend on My love for you; it is always there, never depleted, and perfect." I continued rocking Carl in the darkness and thought my heart was going to erupt with joy. I could not get my mind around the kind of love God has for me.*

Think about the strongest, most powerful love you have ever felt. Maybe it was for a spouse, a child, a parent, or a friend. Sit with that just a minute and then remind yourself that God loves you more than that, far more than anything you have ever felt or can fathom.

Oh, how we long for you to get, as Shelly did, a fresh glimpse of God's deep, passionate, good love for you. God adopts *you* as His very own daughter. Ephesians 1:5 says that it gives Him pleasure to make *you* His. He loves *you*. He has chosen *you* and made *you* a part of His family.

A Sacred Wooing

You may be thinking, *It's fine to read all this about God's love, but how do I recognize when He is calling me to Himself?* Sometimes we don't feel His wooing or we are so distracted and busy that we don't hear Him. The Enemy of your soul doesn't want you to live loved. He will use everything in his arsenal to block God's call to you.

Mimi:

I was speaking at a weeklong conference when a middle-aged Russian woman indicated through a translator that she wanted some individual time with me. She chose a place to meet in a secluded area of the hotel. As we settled in, she told me her story.

She had entered an arranged marriage at fifteen years of age. Her deep resentment about her situation had kept her from expressing or receiving love. She asked me if it was too late to learn to love her husband. I asked her if she knew what would touch her heart, what would woo her. She had no idea, had never even thought about it. She was emotionally frozen.

Many of us are like this woman. We do not know what would break through the frozen sections of our hearts and help us experience God's love for us personally. How do we begin? The God that created you knows you better than anyone; He can show you what would delight your heart. Talk to Him about what you need from Him. Ask Him and wait expectantly for Him to show you. Ask Him to help you experience His Holy Spirit romancing you. As you read the Bible, look for God's love calls to your heart.

As Shelly mentioned earlier, one of the ways God woos us is through the creation He puts around us. Each evening the lavish splash of color and exquisite detail of the clouds in the setting sun is His love declaration to you, if you'll receive it. A tiny flower beside a path, even a weed struggling up through a crack in the cement, can be a reminder of the Creator's love for you. A tree covered with tiny, fragrant blossoms can be just a part of the scenery, or it can speak of God's love to your heart. As you stand there with your nose buried in the flowers, breathing in the sweet fragrance, you can say to your heavenly Lover, "You put this in my path! You know what joy this brings to my heart. Thank You."

God often clothes Himself in others and uses people to be His hands and feet of love in our lives. We can receive the open trust and generosity of a child as a touch of love from His hand. The sound of laughter coming from our loved ones is God's love speaking to us. Someone's hand on our shoulder, a shared look, a heartfelt "How are you?" are all ways He reaches out to us in love. The smile of a stranger, a thoughtful gesture, an unexpected consideration — all these, when viewed through the filter of God's loving call to our hearts, can fill our hearts with His love for us.

When you feel His love, be sure to look from the gift into the face of the Lover of your soul. Take time to express how you feel so that you note and remember God's personal touches.

A Love You Can Be Sure Of

Parents of adopted children sometimes wonder if their kids will worry that their parents might "give them away," as their birth mothers did. Many of us have similar fears when it comes to our status as children of God. We wonder, *Will God decide that He doesn't want me after all? Can I do something that would make Him stop loving me?*

Mimi:

During a conference in South America, an older woman asked to speak to me. I had heard of her amazing work for God. Numerous people had come to Christ through her ministry, and she had served faithfully for many long years. It was late at night when we sat down in a darkened room. She began to sob as she told me the heaviest burden of her heart. She said that all her life, she had been tortured by doubts as to whether she was truly saved. She had never been sure of God's love for her. She was terrified that all she was doing for God might not be enough to earn her place in heaven.

I said to her, "Did your daughter ever nestle deep into your arms with her little hand gripping your blouse? Who was holding who? Could she have held on if you had taken your arms away? Of course not. No matter how tightly her little fingers gripped you, she could never have supported her own weight. That's the way it is with us. We think we are gripping tightly, struggling to hold on to God, but it is God who, in His eternal love, holds us. We don't hold Him."

Life had taught this woman to be wary of love. Has it taught you the same? Do you think you have to earn affection? This woman had never known unconditional love, and she projected the failures of the human love she had known onto God. Have you done that too? "Very few of us really know what it means to be held in the grip of the love of God. We tend to be controlled simply by our own experience."[5] Mimi's friend could not depend on God's love until she stopped looking at it through her earthly experience. Nor can you, but you can trust the character of your heavenly Lover. And when you open up your heart to Him, He will sweep you off your feet.

"[We] pray that you, being rooted and established in love, may have power, together with all the saints, to grasp how wide and long and high and deep is the love of Christ, and to know this love that surpasses knowledge — that you may be filled to the measure of all the fullness of God" (Ephesians 3:17-19).

Holy Habits

- Verse to memorize: "The LORD your God is with you, he is mighty to save. He will take great delight in you, he will quiet you with his love, he will rejoice over you with singing" (Zephaniah 3:17).

- When you celebrate Communion, as you eat the bread and drink the wine or juice, remind yourself that you are receiving into your body symbols of His love for you. Invite Him to speak His love into "the members of your body" (Romans 6:13, NASB), even down to the cells. As you take Communion, thank God for sending Jesus to die and for showing His love to you through His Son.

- Sit and let God love you. Learn to "soak up the luxury of being cherished."[6] Give God a period of time where you do nothing but let Him cover you with His love.

- When you hear a love song, listen to it as if God were singing it to you. Remember that the very Creator of music sings over you. Love songs can make us sad. When we hear them, they may remind us that we don't have anyone who loves us or that our spouse or boyfriend doesn't love us that way. Listen to love songs through the filter of God's love for you, and let the truth of His love fill you.

- Regularly pray Paul's prayer in Ephesians 3:17-19. You can personalize it like this:

  > I pray that I will sink my roots down and be firmly established in God's love. May I have power together with others who believe to grow in my understanding of how wide and long and high and deep the love of Christ really is. And I ask that I may have some knowing of this love that goes beyond anything I can understand and that I will be filled to the brim with all that God is.

- Choose a plant that you see each day to serve as a reminder to pray that you will be rooted and established in God's love.

Responding to His Word

1. Read 1 John 4:7-14. Explain how, according to the passage, God's love is shown to you and how you can reflect that to others.

2. How can you depend on God's love in you to help you love others? Who would you like to show that to? How will you do it?

3. What does 1 John 4:7-14 say that confirms that God lives in you? How can that help you love others?

4. Read John 14:15-27. Make a list of what God does for you out of love. List what you can do in response.

5. Why is there no fear in love, according to 1 John 4:18? How can you allow God's love to address your fears? How would you use this passage to encourage Mimi's friend who doubted her salvation?

6. Explain why John 17:2-3 is so full of wonder for the true believer. Remember that Christ came to reveal the Father's heart.

7. In Lamentations 3:21, Jeremiah says, "This I call to mind and therefore I have hope." What does he call to mind (see verses 22-33)? Why would it give him hope? Note how the love of God and His goodness are linked in this passage.

8. How can the truths you have mined from the above Scriptures help you depend on God's love?

9. Psalm 107:43 says, "They will see in our history the faithful love of the LORD" (NLT). How have you seen God's faithful love in your history? How can that help you depend on Him for the future?

10. Read 1 John 3:1-3,16. What does lavished mean to you? How do you see God lavishing His love on you? Write a prayer of praise and worship for the truth of these verses.

Chapter 5

Guilt-Free and Spiritually Whole

Several months ago, we saw a news story with a riveting photograph of a dead thirteen-foot Burmese python with an alligator hanging out of its side. According to the article, the snake had grown so enormous because he had been feeding on alligators in the Florida Everglades, which have multiplied in abundance since hovering on the verge of extinction just a few decades ago. Apparently the python in the photo had attacked and swallowed the six-foot alligator while it was still alive and the alligator had eaten or clawed its way through the python's side. The alligator had literally killed the snake from the inside out.[1]

This is a graphic picture of what happens to us when we don't address sin and guilt in our lives. Sins are the actions we commit and the attitudes we hold that violate God's character. For example, selfishness versus love, untruth versus truth, betrayal versus faithfulness, uncaring versus compassion, and so on. Often these actions and attitudes come with guilt, the sense that we have done something wrong. But God does not intend for us to take sin or guilt into ourselves. He knows that if they remain in us, like that live alligator, they will kill us spiritually, from the inside out, and keep us from being able to experience the goodness of God.

God's holiness, which is another aspect of His goodness, absolves us of our sin and guilt and also enables us to live a life of holiness. To better understand what we mean when we say God is holy, let's look at how God dealt with two men in the Old Testament named Uzziah and Isaiah.

God's Holiness Versus Our Goodness

Uzziah was a good king of Israel, faithful to God (see 2 Kings 15:3). He was the ultimate authority in Israel, and some of his people even believed he was a god. Because he was so good, Uzziah assumed he had special access to God and was therefore exempt from the law. He defied God and went into the temple's holy place, where only specially prepared priests were permitted. Josephus, the ancient historian, described what happened next: "While [Uzziah] spoke . . . the earth began to shake and the temple split open. A bright shaft of sunlight shone though the opening and fell on the king's face which instantly became leprous."[2] That day Uzziah learned that regardless of how good he was, he was not above God's law. He also discovered that he was not to treat the holiness of the Most High God carelessly. The price for his arrogance was leprosy, and consequently he was forced to live separate from his family, adoring subjects, and the temple of God until he died (see 2 Chronicles 26:21).

Israel had had its share of bad kings, but with Uzziah in leadership, nationally and spiritually the country was in a great place. And as long as King Uzziah was alive, the prophet Isaiah had an ally, but when he died, Isaiah's future was up in the air. Who knew if the next king would share his beliefs, as Uzziah had? Isaiah had just had his legs knocked out from underneath him from the shock of Uzziah's death when he described what he saw in heaven:

In the year that King Uzziah died, I saw the Lord seated on a throne, high and exalted, and the train of his robe filled the temple. Above

him were seraphs, each with six wings: With two wings they covered
their faces, with two they covered their feet, and with two they were
flying. And they were calling to one another:
"Holy, holy, holy is the LORD Almighty;
the whole earth is full of his glory." (Isaiah 6:1-3)

Isaiah was overwhelmed with God's holiness, with His moral
perfection. Isaiah described God as "high and lifted up" (verse 1,
NKJV), meaning that he saw God as transcendent, beyond thought or
comprehension. In other words, God's holiness cannot be compared
to even the best person you know. As humans, we can achieve only
goodness — we can never achieve perfection. God's holiness is perfect,
unique, without limit, uncreated, everlasting, and self-sufficient. We
would live in constant terror of the power of God's holiness if it were
not for His goodness that accompanies every aspect of who He is.

In his vision, Isaiah saw six-winged seraphs, or powerful angels.[3]
Two wings covered their faces, presumably to protect them from the
intensity of God's holiness. Imagine the power of God's holiness: If
seraphs, who have not sinned, cannot look on it, how can we? They also
had two wings covering their feet. Some scholars think that because
in the ancient world feet were considered to be contaminated, they
needed to be covered from the absolute purity of God's presence.

This passage offers us a peek at God's holiness that is similar to
what we see when we look at the sun with a pinhole camera that casts
an image of the sun on a piece of paper. If we were to look directly at the
sun, we would destroy our eyes. The image we can see with a pinhole
camera is faint. That is all that our limited vision and understanding
can grasp. Just as we cannot possibly look directly at the sun or grasp
its totality, were we to come eyeball to eyeball with all of God's holiness, it would burn us up.

Because God is absolutely holy, He cannot stand our sin. A
common thread in definitions of holiness is the idea of being set apart.

A holy article is something that is "set apart" for religious purposes. A holy life is "set apart" from worldly standards. But even a holy person is only partially holy, partially set apart. Only God is wholly holy, so He is wholly set apart. His separation from us is infinite.

What About My Sin and Guilt?

Perhaps you're thinking, *Thanks, Mimi and Shelly! I thought I was feeling guilty before, but this talk of God's holiness makes me feel even guiltier! Maybe Isaiah felt forgiven, but he was a prophet. He never did the kind of things I have done. If God can't stand sin, then He must not be able to stand me, because even though I am a Christian, I still struggle with* _____ (fill in the blank with whatever sins you wrestle with).

If you're thinking anything like that, we're so sorry. And God is sorry too, because God's holiness not only convicts us of the sin, it is also the remedy for our sin. Without the conviction, we would never know our need, and without the remedy, we would never have hope of anything but eternal separation.

Prior to Uzziah's death, Isaiah had been pronouncing dire consequences on people because of their sin. "Woe to you," he announced repeatedly (Isaiah 5:5,8,11,20-22). But his attitude changed after he saw into the throne room of heaven and faced God's holiness. When Isaiah realized the purity of God's holiness and the deep contrast of his puny goodness to God's, he saw his own sinfulness. There was nothing he could say or hang on to in his own defense. He declared, "Woe to me! . . . I am ruined!" (Isaiah 6:5).

God didn't expose Isaiah's sinfulness to ruin him or to humiliate him; he did it to teach him that no mortal, not even a prophet, could enjoy relationship with God without His intervention. It's interesting to note that nobody had accused Isaiah of any sin, yet when he saw God's holiness, he felt convicted. Romans 2:4 tells us that God's goodness leads us to repent or turn our backs on sin and turn toward Him. One of the foundational tenets of the goodness of God is that He wants relationship with us.

Throughout Scripture, God provides a way for us to "see" Him. Isaiah saw God "high and lifted up" because God allowed him that experience. God responded to Isaiah's admission of guilt and sin by sending an angel to minister grace to Isaiah. Imagine a six-winged creature flying at you, carrying a red-hot coal! At face value, it surely didn't seem like a ministry of grace; it was terrifying. Author David Needham says, "Can you imagine Isaiah's terror? No place to hide! No alternative but death itself. He knew his impurity could not coexist in the presence of God's spotlessness."[4] But God did not intend to hurt Isaiah with the coal. His purpose was to heal him, to remove Isaiah's guilt and sin so he could enjoy a full relationship with Him. As the seraph touched Isaiah's lips with the burning coal, powerful words flowed from him: "Your guilt is taken away and your sin atoned for" (Isaiah 6:7). What joy! Isaiah's sin was forgiven and his guilt removed.

God could have allowed our ungodliness to forever be a barrier that separates us from Him. But in His goodness, He has made a way for us to enjoy an intimate relationship with Him. Yet, despite having accepted Jesus' provision for their sin, many Christians continue to carry the guilt of that sin. When we do that, we are not spiritually whole and we are focused on ourselves. How can we experience spiritual wholeness, which is freedom from sin and guilt? By responding to and then embracing His holiness.

By Responding to His Holiness

Jesus says in Matthew 5:8 that the pure in heart shall see God. We need to understand that being pure in heart does not mean being without sin. For instance, David, whom Scripture calls "a man after [God's] own heart" (1 Samuel 13:14), struggled with sin. In Psalm 19:13, he prays, "Keep your servant also from willful sins." Rather than being sinless, the spiritually whole are those who choose to consistently seek personal purity by:

- **Purifying the heart.** "Let us draw near to God with a sincere heart in full assurance of faith, having our hearts sprinkled to cleanse us from a guilty conscience" (Hebrews 10:22; see also James 4:8; 1 Timothy 1:5; 2 Timothy 2:22; Hebrews 3:12). Our friend Lilly is a good example of someone choosing to live in purity of heart. Every morning she makes sure that her heart is right with God. She confesses anything she knows of that keeps her from intimacy with Him. Lilly daily asks Him to show her the heart attitudes she needs to release to God in order to walk in purity with Him.

- **Purifying the mind.** "To be made new in the attitude of your minds" (Ephesians 4:23; see also Romans 7:23; 12:2). Pat is working on changing her thinking patterns. She wants to be made new in her mind by turning her complaining into gratefulness. In order to purify her mind, she confesses her ungrateful spirit and prays daily that God will help her recognize when she slips into old mental habits as she actively cultivates a mindset of gratitude.

- **Purifying the lips.** "Put away perversity from your mouth; keep corrupt talk far from your lips" (Proverbs 4:24; see also Job 33:3; Psalm 34:13; Colossians 3:8; Proverbs 12:14). Because she knows that "out of the overflow of [the] heart [the] mouth speaks" (Luke 6:45), our friend Kate started the process of purifying her speech by asking God to cleanse her heart and thoughts. She began to work on controlling the impulsive reactions in her heart and mind by reining them in and replacing them with truth and godly thoughts. She discovered that the more she did that internal exercise, the more she was able to keep her tongue from running away with her in public.

- **Purifying the hands.** "Who may ascend the hill of the LORD? Who may stand in his holy place? He who has clean hands and a pure heart" (Psalm 24:3-4; see also Ephesians 2:10). Before starting each day, Ella, a mother of three young children, offers her hands to God, asking Him to help her touch others in a way that conveys the inward tenderness of her heart for God. The expression of both our lips and our hands are outward signs of the inward state of the heart.

You may have noticed that the four areas of purity flow from one another. As we clean up our hearts (our core) with God's help and replace sin with His purity, we can also purify our minds. Speech flows out of our heart and mind, and what we do — the work of our hands — is a tangible reflection of what goes on inside us.

The purity and cleansing that God calls for can be achieved only through His power and His Word. Psalm 119:9 asks, "How can a [woman] keep [her] way pure?" The answer to that question is, "By living according to His Word." Verse 11 adds to that because it tells us that when we have God's Word in our hearts, it will keep us from sin.

However, sometimes we experience guilt over things that the Bible doesn't specifically address as a sin. When that's the case, what are we to do?

Shelly:

I'd been meeting with Inga for several weeks when she asked me whether a particular issue in her life was a sin. She wasn't sure because it was something the Bible doesn't specifically address. She had asked several other Christians the same question. Some had told her the issue was a sin; others had told her it wasn't. And now she wanted to know what I thought.

*I gulped. If the Bible is not specific on whether something is sin,
I am careful about giving an opinion. So I took Inga to the verse
that God uses with me when I want to know if something does not
please Him. "A [woman] is a slave to whatever has mastered [her]"
(2 Peter 2:19). I asked her, does this issue master you or do you
control it? If something enslaves us or masters us — if we can't stop
doing it — then it is sin.*

*I gave her a simple example from my life. Sometimes when it
snows on a weekday and I turn on the television to find out if the
kids have a snow day or a school delay, I can't seem to manage to
turn off the television. It plays, distractingly, in the background all
day long. Because I cannot turn it off, the television masters me; I
am a slave to it. I must ask God's forgiveness and strength to not be
mastered by the television.*

God makes us holy when we turn away from our sin. Second
Timothy 2:21 says, "If a [woman] cleanses [herself] . . . , [she] will be
an instrument for noble purposes, made holy, useful to the Master and
prepared to do any good work."

Not only does God forgive and purify us from our personal wrongdoing, He wants to cleanse us from anything that keeps us from being
holy, like He is. That includes the guilt that often accompanies sin.

Embracing His Holiness

When God forgives sin, He also wants to remove the guilt of it. God
freed Isaiah from both the sin and the weight of its guilt. Isn't it interesting that Isaiah was a prophet, chosen by God to be His voice to the
people of Israel, yet he too knew guilt?

God's way has always been to separate the sin and the guilt from the
sinner. He wants to pull the poison away from your cleansed heart. The
Old Testament institution of the scapegoat demonstrates this. Each year

the sins of all the Israelites were symbolically placed onto a goat — the scapegoat — and the animal was led away from camp, never to return (see Leviticus 16:20-22). This symbolism was to remind the Israelites that God separated their sin from them. Micah 7:29 tells us that God hurls our sins into the depths of the sea. Revelation 21:1 says that in the new earth there will be "no longer any sea." The Judge of all the earth is saying, "I will not leave any evidence of your sin. You are free."

Christ's death on the cross was an act of judicial justice, but it also removed our guilt so that we could enjoy relational wholeness with God. When we remember our sin and carry the guilt of it, we are not spiritually whole. Sin from the past is like a large, heavy bag that we drag around from one day to the next, even as it continues to grow. Satan is so crafty that he makes us initially believe that sin is no big deal, but as soon as we give in to it, he lowers the guilt bomb and continually condemns us for it, even after we've asked God to forgive us. Satan does not want us to know the relief of guilt removed.

If we have been forgiven, why do we still feel guilty? Scripture is clear that God forgives us, but even so, we find it hard to let go of the disappointment we have in ourselves. It hurts God when we do that. He paid the ultimate price to remove sin and guilt from us. He doesn't want us to carry that stain. So why do we? Because we usually hold high standards for ourselves and our behavior. When we fall short and aren't holy or good, we become disappointed in ourselves. We think, *I shouldn't have done that. I can't stand the fact that I blew it. I'm better than that.* With those thoughts, Satan gets us in a place where we think that feeling bad about what we have done is the "right" attitude to have. This is actually a form of inverted pride. Satan has gotten us to focus on ourselves. We subconsciously believe the lie that we really are too good to have done what we did. That guilt keeps us from enjoying the holiness of God and intimacy with Him.

If we have confessed our sin to God yet continue to live with guilt, it is as if we are saying, "God forgives me, but I can't forgive myself."

That is double-mindedness. James 1:8 tells us that a double-minded person is unstable in everything she does. The question that biblical counselors are most often asked is, "How do I forgive myself?" If this is your question, go back to the basics. Remind yourself of the truth: You have been cleansed from your sin and are free of any guilt. Scripture clearly states, "If we confess our sins, he is faithful and just and will forgive us our sins and purify us from *all* unrighteousness" (1 John 1:9, emphasis added). God extends His forgiveness to all who ask. It is our choice whether we will believe that and accept the finished work that Jesus did on our behalf.

You also need to remind yourself of another truth: "The heart is deceitful . . . and desperately wicked; who can know it?" (Jeremiah 17:9, NKJV). Like Isaiah, you are fully capable of every evil thing. You need to understand that you could sin again. That's why you need Jesus. That's why all of us need the holiness He offered to us through the cross. We hurt God when we've confessed our sin but continue to feel ashamed when we grieve and wallow in our failure.

God says, "I, even I, am he who blots out your transgressions, for my own sake, and remembers your sins no more" (Isaiah 43:25). Jesus went to the cross to wipe out our sin. He doesn't remember it, yet we keep carrying it around. The significance of the statement "For my own sake" leaves us breathless with wonder. How could it be that God forgives our sin for *His* sake? He forgives us because He wants to. Forgiveness comes out of His holy heart, which is full of goodness. God reaches into Himself and gladly pays the debt of our sin so that He might have the joy of intimacy with us. It is not our "right" living that triggers this response in God; it is His holy goodness.

If you struggle with guilt because you continue to revisit your sin and the devastation it caused, you need to acknowledge that yes, you sinned, and yes, you could do it again. Agree with the truth that you are fully capable of all that you have done and more. Then declare this truth:

*I am forgiven and God no longer holds it against me. I praise God
that I am a new person in Christ. God provides everything I need to
live a holy life.*[5]

The promise in Isaiah 61:2-4 is that God will comfort all of us
who mourn over our sin, and He will replace it with a crown of beauty
instead. Our sin is simply ashes, and we cannot take it back or change
it. When we persist in feeling guilty, it keeps us from God's holy plan
for our lives. He wants to take the ashes of our past and give us the oil
of gladness in return. We can put on a spirit of praise instead of feeling
guilty over what we have done. When we praise Him, it puts our focus
back on Him and His holiness.

God can rebuild and restore the damage of our sin (see chapter 10).
He says, "I am rebuilding the devastation and repairing the desolation
of many generations" (Isaiah 61:4, our paraphrase). Then He declares
us useful for His service: "You will be called priests of the LORD, you
will be named ministers of our God" (verse 6). He affirms that promise
in the New Testament as well: "You are a chosen people, a royal priesthood, a holy nation, a people belonging to God" (1 Peter 2:9).

Keep in mind that even when we live in holiness, our minds still
remember the things we've done or that have happened to us. Satan
can bring those thoughts and feelings back into our conscious mind
at any moment. When we remember our past, we are tempted to take
on guilt. But we don't have to. We can declare to the Enemy, "I am
chosen by God to be holy, a new person. He does not remember my
wrongdoing. I am not associated anymore with that sin." Satan will get
tired of bringing it back to your mind when he meets with that kind
of response. A. W. Tozer says, "Any belief that does not command the
one who holds it is not a real belief."[6] When we stand on the truth and
promises of God, the guilt and memories of our past lose their power
and cannot rule over us.

Romans 2:4 tells us that it is God's goodness that leads us to repent. Did you get that? He leads us to repent — to turn our backs on sin and turn toward Him, to choose holiness — because He is good. When sin and guilt have no power over us, we are free to live in holiness. Our good, holy God longs for a personal, intimate relationship with us. First Corinthians 1:9 tells us, "God . . . has called you into fellowship with his Son Jesus Christ our Lord." We fulfill the purpose He created us for when we enjoy relationship with God.

A Redeemed Nature

God has also commanded us to "be holy, for I am holy" (Leviticus 11:44, NASB). What does it mean for us to be holy as God is holy? It means to be spiritually whole, free from sin, pure in heart, godly and guiltless. The goal of living a holy life is to become like Christ (see Romans 8:29), making intimate relationship with the One in whose image we are made an integral part of us, making Christlikeness the essence of who we are.

This command would be impossible and condemning if God had not already provided everything we need to fulfill it. "His divine power has given us everything we need for life and godliness through . . . him who called us by his . . . goodness" (2 Peter 1:3). The solution for our sin and guilt has to come from God Himself because only He can make us holy. God through Jesus Christ cleared the way for you to be made holy as He is. Christ died to redeem your entire nature, not just to forgive your individual sins. He didn't just die for the lie you told or the adultery you committed; He died to redeem you from your very nature as a liar or an adulterer.

Imagine a patient who has terrible migraines due to a brain tumor. The doctor can give her an aspirin for her headaches or he can perform brain surgery and remove the tumor that causes them. Similarly, God doesn't just treat the symptoms of our sin but the cause. He who first made us good wants to heal us of our sin and its effects so that we can enjoy unhindered relationship with Him.

Because God is good, He does not ask us to be holy and then leave us to figure it out on our own. We have a friend who works with the profoundly deaf. She teaches them to live and speak in a hearing world with the use of hearing aids. Even though the hearing aids are the best the world has to offer, they require regular calibration. Normal use throws off the efficiency of even the top-of-the-line machine's fine-tuning. It is similar with our souls. Our nature has been redeemed — made new — but "daily use" throws us out of calibration.

Practical Holiness

The practical outworking of God's holiness in our lives begins by living with Him as our standard, or our plumb line. When we line ourselves up with His holiness, we can clearly see how far short we are and what attitudes and actions we cannot allow in our lives. In a world of moral decline, increased terrorism, and growing uncertainty, we find great security in aligning ourselves with a holy, unchanging, and good God. When we read in the Bible about what He calls us to, it shows us where we need a course correction.

Here's an example of how this works. One morning at her weekly Bible study, Lisa teased one of her friends about the answer she gave to one of the questions. After class, the more Lisa thought about it, the more convinced she became that she had hurt her friend. But she thought, *I didn't mean to hurt her. I was just trying to be funny.* She kept remembering, with guilt, the look of hurt on her friend's face but rationalized it away. Then one morning while reading the Sermon on the Mount, Lisa read, "If you are offering your gift at the altar and there remember that your brother has something against you, leave your gift there in front of the altar. First go and be reconciled to your brother; then come and offer your gift" (Matthew 5:23-24). She realized that if she didn't address the problem with her friend, her gift of worship would not be sweet to God. God showed Lisa that it was standing in the way of her relationship with Him, of her being holy as He is. Lisa asked God to forgive her for hurting her friend. Then she called her friend and asked her to forgive her for how she had treated her at the Bible study. Like Lisa, when we spend time in His Word, we can get a fresh "reading" to chart our course. God's instructions for life are what we use to recalibrate our lives for holy living.

Hebrews 12:14 calls us to make every effort to perfect holiness. The apostle Paul said, "Since we have these promises, dear friends, let us purify ourselves from everything that contaminates body and spirit, perfecting holiness out of reverence for God" (2 Corinthians 7:1). These passages make it clear that holy living requires effort on our part. Perfecting holiness sounds difficult and ominous, but it simply means that we collaborate with God to continue the process of becoming spiritually whole, of living free from the grip of sin and guilt.

To become holy, we must turn from our sin and turn to godliness. We see the concept of turning from and turning to in Matthew 12:43-45:

> *When an evil spirit comes out of a man, it goes through arid places seeking rest and does not find it. Then it says, "I will return to the house I left." When it arrives, it finds the house unoccupied, swept clean and put in order. Then it goes and takes with it seven other spirits more wicked than itself, and they go in and live there. And the final condition of that man is worse than the first.*

Carla experienced the truth of these verses. She was in and out of drug rehabilitation repeatedly. Even though she knew that she was in jeopardy of losing her children, every time, within a few weeks of release, she fell back into doing drugs. The fourth time she went to rehab, Carla had little hope for change, but she came out transformed and has been sober for years. When asked what made the difference, Carla replied, "Every time you go for treatment, they take your drugs away from you, but they don't give you anything in their place. This last time, they took my drugs and gave me Jesus instead. That made the difference." To break her habit, Carla had to not only turn from the drugs but replace them with something else.

You may be thinking, *I've already turned to Jesus, but I still need help to live a holy life!* If so, understand that this principle is true for any lifestyle change. Ephesians 4 and 5 provide examples of what we must turn from and turn to. For instance, it says, "Put to death . . . rid yourself . . . take off." How would you put something undesirable to death? Or rid yourself? Or take off? Don't feed it. Starve it. Turn your back on it. Pay no attention. The problem is that if we say we won't pay attention to something, we usually end up fixating on it unless we focus on something else. God knows that, so He teaches us to turn to His goodness as we turn from our sin.

Think of it like this: The growing season in Colorado is short. As soon as there is the faintest whiff of spring in the air, we get the ground ready to plant flowers and herbs. To do that, we have to prepare the soil and remove all the weeds, the stones, and anything else that would keep the plants from having their best shot at flourishing. That's the same principle in perfecting holiness. We rid ourselves of anything that stands in the way of God doing His work in us. We provide Him with fertile soil in our hearts so that His holiness can take root and produce a bumper crop.

God's purpose is for you to live in spiritual wholeness. That is why Christ died. "Christ loved the church and gave himself up for her to make her holy . . . and to present her to himself as a radiant church, without stain or wrinkle or any other blemish, but holy and blameless" (Ephesians 5:25-27). There is nothing you can do to be more worthy of forgiveness, but there is much you can and must do if you want to embrace the journey toward personal holiness and intimacy with our good God. He makes it possible for you to be what He meant you to be.

Holy, good God, thank You for forgiving our sin and taking away our guilt. Thank You for doing everything necessary so that we can live in intimate relationship with You! We want You to occupy every part of us, from the top of our head to the tips of our toes. Show us any resistance to Your good work of making us holy. Help us recognize what we need to turn away from and quickly turn to You and Your character. We want to be holy as You called us to be.

Holy Habits

- Verses to memorize: "Put off your old self, which is being corrupted by its deceitful desires; to be made new in the attitude of your minds; and to put on the new self, created to be like God in true righteousness and holiness" (Ephesians 4:22-24).

- Designate a small spot in your home or office to represent the circle of God's holy goodness — for example, a place in a hallway that the sun shines on each morning. Take a moment each day, especially when you are tempted to carry guilt, and stand in that spot. Thank God that He has atoned for your sin and taken away your guilt.

- Choose a verse that addresses a particular area of guilt you have carried. Memorize it and repeat the truth of it over and over to get it down into your heart. When guilty feelings attempt to overtake you, quote the verse.

- Ask God what you have that you can set apart or make holy for His service (see Zechariah 14:20; Isaiah 23:18). Because being "wholly holy" involves all aspects of your life, go around your home and set apart the ordinary, normal things for God.

As you use those things, choose to be conscious of the fact that you have given them over to God's holiness. For example, Mimi went to an office store and had a stamp made that said, "Holy to the Lord." Then she stamped everything that she uses in everyday life, even her car. She went from room to room in her house and gave all those things to God.

- Invite God to occupy you and remove all resistance you may have to His work of holiness in your life: "Offer the parts of your body to him as instruments of righteousness" (Romans 6:13). First Thessalonians 5:23 calls us to allow God to "sanctify you through and through." For instance, you might pray regularly that He will fill every cell of your body and show you any area where you are resisting His work.

- Consciously choose to turn *from* something and *to* holiness. Amy Carmichael writes that famous author and preacher F. B. Meyer was grouchy when he was young. He told her that:

> he had found relief from this very thing by look-
> ing up the moment he felt it coming, and saying,
> "Thy sweetness, Lord." . . . Take the oppo-
> site of your temptation and look up inwardly,
> naming that opposite; . . . Impatience — Thy
> patience, Lord; Selfishness — Thy unselfishness,
> Lord; . . . Resentment, inward heat, fuss — Thy sweet-
> ness Lord, Thy calmness, Thy peacefulness.[7]

Follow Dr. Meyer's example and turn *from* the ugliness — before it starts — *to* His character worked out through you.

Responding to His Word

1. What did you think of the story of the python and the alligator? List some of the ways that sin and guilt can "kill" us.

2. Read Isaiah 6:1-9. Try to put yourself in Isaiah's shoes. How would you feel in that situation?

3. In Isaiah 6:5, Isaiah cries out, "Woe to me!" Previously he had been crying out, "Woe to you," to the people around him. What changed his focus? How could an awareness of God's holiness make you say, "Woe to me"?

4. After Isaiah recognized his unworthiness to interact with God, verse 6 describes his cleansing. Why do you think God had the seraphs use a burning coal? What does it mean that Isaiah's guilt has been removed and that his sin is atoned for?

5. Isaiah 6:8 is God's appeal and Isaiah's response. Before God asks, "Whom shall I send?" several things happened. Why do you think that series of events would be important before Isaiah could answer God? What does it say about what needs to happen in you before you respond to God's call on your life?

6. Review the sections on purity of heart and mind (see page 82) and read the suggested verses. Summarize the truth of the verses for those two areas.

7. Review the sections on purity of lips and hands (see pages 82-83) and read the verses. Summarize the scriptural truth for those areas that need cleansing.

8. Read Isaiah 53:1-12. Note what each verse tells you about what God did for you. When you finish your list, thank Him.

9. God's perfect holiness provides us with a new nature out of which we can live without guilt. Read and summarize the truth of the following passages: Psalm 34:5; 31:1; Romans 9:33; 10:11; 1 Peter 2:6.

10. Read Ephesians 4:22-32. Make a simple table of the things that passage tells us to turn from and turn to.

Turn From	Turn To

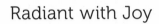

Chapter 6

Radiant with Joy

Donna has suffered from severe rheumatoid arthritis since childhood. She has endured multiple surgeries on her hands and feet, resulting in the loss of nearly all her joints. Yet that doesn't keep her from enjoying life and exuding joy. She sits with dignity in her wheelchair, her hands resting lifelessly on the arms. When she is around other people, her attention is on everybody else, her face radiant as she interacts in lively conversation. Her enthusiasm does not reflect her constant pain or other enormous physical difficulties.

What is the secret of Donna's joy? According to her friends, she has made it a lifelong practice to focus on God's goodness. You can't be around her and not witness the outward evidence of her inward determination to see His joyful goodness.

Can you imagine trying to live without any joints in your fingers and toes and with constant pain? How would you manage ordinary life? Donna (whose middle name happens to be Joy!) faces those challenges and many others while overflowing with joy. The root of her joy is her life with God and her determination to live in His goodness. She reflects the truth that God is full of joy in the depths of His being, and all of creation magnifies that joy. She basks in her position in Christ and radiates that reality, despite her physical limitations. Her example reminds us that there is a deep, radiant joy that cannot be found in circumstances or things.

Yet many Christians spend a lifetime going to church and trying to be obedient but never come close to experiencing this kind of joy. We suspect that this might be due to their view of God.

How Do You See God?

What words come to mind when you think of God? When we asked a group of women this question, they said such things as:

- Severe
- Powerful
- Holy
- Sovereign
- Loving

Not one of these women said they think of joy when they think of God. They are not alone. In our experience, most Christians don't think about joy as being a part of God's character. Some see Him as a killjoy — that He spends His time scouring our lives for sin or that because He hates sin, He must feel disappointed with His creation, at least most of the time. Sadly, for many, Christianity seems to be more about what we should not do and be than about who we could be and what we can have in Him.

Oh, how we have missed God's heart because, you see, part of God's essence is joy. It fills His heart, and He wants it to spill over onto His creation. Do you long to be joyful no matter what life brings your way? If so, we have good news for you. It's been said that we become like that upon which we gaze. If you gaze upon God, you will become more like Him. You will become more joy-filled.

Full of Joy

One way to gaze upon God is to study His character as seen in the Bible. Have you ever noticed all the passages that talk about joy? Depending on the translation you use, there are nearly 550 references to joy. The Old and New Testaments both depict God as being full of joy. His joy is not a temporary, fleeting, emotional high; it is a sense of well-being that endures through both good and bad days.

Life becomes disappointing and dark when we don't get what we want. Joy comes from letting go of our human, natural desires and giving them to God. As we yield ourselves to Him, we come to a point where we love Him so much that His desires become ours. That is a direct result of being in communion with God. Then we know the satisfaction of our soul — real joy!

Let's take a closer look at God's desires and what fills His heart with joy:

The work of His hands. Each day, God looked at what He created and saw that "it was good." He could have used words such as *pleasant, beautiful, excellent, lovely, delightful,* and *joyful* to describe what He made. But He didn't. God was delighted by His creation, and the stars and angels reflected that delight: "The morning stars sang together and all the angels shouted for joy" (Job 38:7). Creation didn't happen in silence. Far from it. Wouldn't you like to hear the music those morning stars made to accompany God's joyful creation? "The secret of the universe is this shout of joy. God says 'You are aware that ecstasy is the cornerstone and foundation of everything.'"[1]

Take a moment and imagine God standing back, looking at Mount Everest, and saying, "Wow, that's good!" He said that about everything He made, including you! Do you believe it? Do you believe that when God made you, you delighted Him? He created you while the stars sang and the angels shouted. He was brimming with joy, and He said, "Wow, she's good!" Sit with that thought for a while. Ask God to let the truth of it seep deep into your soul. When it does, it will fill your heart with joy to know that the Lord of the Universe not only loves you but also delights in you!

What are some of the things you delight in? Have you ever cooked a particularly delicious meal and been gratified by how much your family or guests enjoyed it? Have you successfully taken on a challenge? Have you ever done something kind for someone else that encouraged or inspired that person? Just as you enjoy the works of your hands, so does our good and joyful God.

When goodness is expressed with joy, it enhances its quality. It's one thing to do something for another because you have to do it; it's another to do it joyfully because you want to. A woman may have a good heart, but add the element of joy to her actions, and her goodness takes on a new and exciting dimension.

We saw this firsthand in our dear friend Rosa. She had a humble house in a poor section on the outskirts of Quito, where there were no paved streets. There was nothing easy about her life. After rising long before dawn to cook and clean her simple home and get her children off to school, she would spend several long hours on a crowded bus traveling to her job as a household maid. Her income put food on the table, but there was little if anything left over for clothes, school, and the myriad needs of a growing family.

Still Rosa wanted to show her love for us. She knew how much our families enjoyed being together, so she invited all nine of us for dinner. As she radiantly served us many local delicacies, we could hardly stand it. We knew the meal had cost her a great deal of money and an enormous amount of time to prepare. Her family would have to eat only rice for days to recover from her gift to us, yet we could almost feel the giddy joy in her. Because Rosa's good heart took such great pleasure in providing us an occasion to be together and enjoy rare, special food, we received it gladly. That evening sparkles in our memories. The secret ingredient in those delicious dishes was the joy that Rosa obviously took in preparing and serving them to us.

Rosa never could have been so joyful if her heart had been pinned to earthly satisfaction. She would have hoarded her money, time, and energies. Instead, she had learned to live her life through the perspective of God's joy, and it spilled over onto everything she did.

Exercising forgiveness and redemption. Joy also fills God's heart when He exercises His goodness. " 'I am the LORD, who exercises kindness, justice and righteousness on earth, for in these I delight,' declares the LORD" (Jeremiah 9:24). One of the primary ways God exercises His goodness is through forgiveness and redemption.

Jesus told three short stories in Luke 15 that teach this. In verses 4-7, we read the story of one sheep out of a flock of one hundred who gets lost. The shepherd, who represents Jesus, goes out to find the lost sheep (soul) and bring it back to His Father. In that short passage, there are three references to God's joy:

When he finds [the sheep], he joyfully puts it on his shoulders and goes home. Then he calls his friends and neighbors together and says, "Rejoice with me; I have found my lost sheep." I tell you that in the same way there will be more rejoicing in heaven over one sinner who repents than over ninety-nine righteous persons who do not need to repent. (verses 5-7)

Joy fills God's heart when people find their home in Him.

Jesus tells another story with a similar ending and intent. It's about a woman who has ten coins and loses one of them.

When she finds it, she calls her friends and neighbors together and says, "Rejoice with me; I have found my lost coin." In the same way, I tell you, there is rejoicing in the presence of the angels of God over one sinner who repents. (verses 9-10)

Heaven is filled with joy over each soul that repents. Most of us think that this celebration happens only when people give their heart to Christ. However, repentance of sin can be ongoing, and according to this passage, heaven celebrates *every time* we ask God to forgive us. Even though we are fallen beings, we bring Him joy when we turn to Him. Have you ever noticed how many celebrations there are in the Bible? Feasts, weeklong festivals, times of remembering God's goodness. God made joyful celebration a part of His people's worship. He is a God who celebrates and He wants us to rejoice. We can do that because He joyfully lavishes His goodness upon us.

The final parable in Luke 15 tells of a father who waits daily for his wayward son to return home. After searching the road countless times, his heart quickens with anticipation when he finally sees a familiar figure approaching. Not able to contain himself, the father runs to meet his son. With hugs, kisses, and tears, the beaming father brings his lost-and-found son home. To express his joy, the father plans a huge party. When the father explained the reason for the party to his older son, he said, "We *had to celebrate and be glad*, because this brother of yours was dead and is alive again; he was lost and is found" (verse 32, emphasis added).

Each of these stories illustrates God's tenderness, compassion, and joy over the repentant sinner. Each example represents a different state of the heart. In the sheep, we see someone lost and "bewildered; in the lost drachma, the sinner stamped with God's image, but lying lost, useless and ignorant of his own worth; in the prodigal son, the conscious and willing sinner."[2] Regardless of the condition of the soul, a repentant sinner causes great celebration in heaven. God delights to forgive anyone who seeks Him.

"Creation and Redemption are the expression of the overflow of the joy of the Lord."[3] God not only created us with joy but also redeems us in joy.

Every Day a Gift to Experience Joy

The psalmist declared, "This is the day the LORD has made; let us rejoice and be glad in it" (Psalm 118:24). Sadly, many of us — from a human perspective — don't have much to rejoice about. There have been days that have brought us face-to-face with betrayal, rape, divorce, abuse, death, and other horrors. Because of that, we may even dread a new day, fearful of what fresh pain it will bring. How can there be joy in that?

Our daily circumstances cannot be the basis for our joy. The foundation for joy is the belief that God is who He says He is and that He will do what He promises. We have been gripped by the quote "The opposite of joy is not sorrow, it is unbelief."[4] In other words, if we choose to believe what we know to be true about God, He can give us a joy beyond understanding in the middle of every challenge because of who He is in us. "Even though you do not see him now, you *believe* in him and are filled with an *inexpressible* and *glorious joy*" (1 Peter 1:8, emphasis added). We cultivate our belief in who He is and what He does by the study of His Word. It builds a foundation of understanding that we can depend on. "The precepts of the LORD are right, giving joy to the heart" (Psalm 19:8).

It is possible to rejoice every day, not because the day is filled with good things but because the source of all goodness and joy lives in us. He is with us to face whatever comes our way. What a powerful truth! That means that we never encounter a difficulty or a day alone. Because He is a good, joyful God, we can choose to look at every one of our challenges with His help. We can trust Him to have a much broader and higher purpose in mind, to be in control even though we are not. We don't have to go looking for joy; He is resident joy, inexpressible and glorious (see 1 Peter 1:8).

Each day is as glorious to God as the first one He made. It is a fresh exhibit of His joyful, creative Spirit. Have you ever thought about the repetition of the day being God's way of replicating the joy of the previous one? G. K. Chesterton wrote, "Children have abounding vitality. . . . Therefore they want things repeated and unchanged. They always say, 'Do it again.' . . . Grown-up people are not strong enough to exult in monotony. It is possible that God says every morning, 'Do it again' to the sun; and every evening, 'Do it again' to the moon. The repetition in Nature may not be a mere recurrence; it may be a theatrical encore."[5]

Each day brings its own fresh goodness, if we will notice. Jeremiah declared,

> Because of the LORD's great love we are not consumed,
>   for his compassions never fail.
> They are new every morning;
>   great is your faithfulness.
> I say to myself, "The LORD is my portion;
>   therefore I will wait for him." (Lamentations 3:22-24)

In essence, the prophet was saying, "I will notice and remind myself of who God is, that His goodness is new every day, even if my situation threatens to consume me."

You cannot remember something you have never noticed. To sharpen your awareness, you might start each day with this prayer: *Lord, show me Your joyful goodness in this day.* You can delight in its ending as well. Both of us like to invite people over just to enjoy and celebrate the sunset together. We usually prepare our hearts by listening to a worship song and then praying together. We sit on the deck or in front of a big window and watch as the sun sinks behind the horizon. We talk about the colors, clouds, and magnificent artwork of our Creator. Each day joyfully begins and ends with its own special, unique wrapping as a reminder of God's good gift.

Christ tells His Father that He wants a "full measure of my joy within them" (John 17:13). In other words, He prays that every aspect of His joy will be a part of who we are. Real joy comes from the person of Christ living within us, regardless of what is happening in our circumstances. This is vastly different than the best the world has to offer because it is a daily, fresh pouring of Himself through us. We can think of ourselves as open jars and ask Him to fill us: *Give me Your wisdom, Your joy, Your perspective, Your strength today, Father.* He promises that "he will satisfy your needs in a sun-scorched land and will strengthen your frame. You will be like a well-watered garden, like a spring whose waters never fail" (Isaiah 58:11). God limitlessly offers who He is to us each day.

Experiencing His Joy

How do we tap into God's joy? How can it become ours? How can we live in this particular aspect of God's goodness? It will not happen if we give to God only what we think is necessary to produce the desired results. Each morning before we rush into the day, our quiet time may have a familiar ring. We might pray something such as, *Oh, God, give me a quick shot of joy. Today is going to be a challenge.* We will never enjoy the gift of joy from God until we put our whole selves into a special place of relationship. (We'll talk more about what this means in chapter 9.) Real joy comes from walking with God. He puts His Spirit within us, and with the assurance of His joyful presence, we can live in a world of uncertainty and fear and say, "All is well."

But, you may wonder, *how do I do that?* We have to purposefully pay attention to Him by doing the things we've been talking about. The joy of the Lord comes from Him. First Samuel 15:22 tells us, "To obey is better than sacrifice, and to heed [pay attention] is better than the fat of rams." God wants our attention. As we've said, we cannot trust someone we do not know. Only as we grow to know Him more can we begin to understand that deep satisfying joy comes from knowing Him and trusting His purposes for our lives.

Expressing His Joy

Each of us starts every day with access to a fresh, unlimited dose of God's joy. He can give us all we need so that we in turn can share His joy with others.

As we deepen our intimacy with Him, we can access and express joy through our worship. We have often wondered what people would think of God if all they knew about Him was what they learned by observing us in worship. God comments on the lack of sincerity in the worship of the Israelites, "You have not . . . lavished on me the fat of your sacrifices" (Isaiah 43:24). It was as if they were sending God a note on a yellow sticky pad with the word *thanks* printed on the top. By not giving their best, they missed the joy that results from sincere worship. Their worship carried no evidence of love, care, creativity, excitement, or forethought. Our good, joyful Father has supplied us with a wealth of expressions for worship, and He delights to see what we will do with them.

Mary expressed joyful, extravagant worship when she poured expensive ointment on Jesus' feet and wiped the excess with her hair (see John 12:1-7). She did not simply deliver the perfume to Him; she poured it out with her own hands. She showed her love, humility, and esteem of His worth by anointing the lowliest and most common part of Christ's body with the best she had. Her lavish expression of love was punctuated by her lack of self-consciousness in gently wiping His feet with her hair. (A Jewish woman never let her hair down in public.) We are sure that Mary's joy increased as she worshipped.

We can follow her example of extravagant worship. God gave us our bodies as tools to express our hearts. Some of us do that by raising our hands or arms when we sing or pray. Others kneel or lie flat before God. We can sit quietly, bow our heads, run, jump, or dance. Our bodies can communicate what we feel. That means we can do things for other people as a part of our worship — cleaning their home, dropping by with groceries or a meal, caring for their kids, and other things all the while praying, *Lord, because we adore You, let Your joy in us spill out onto others.* Composer Franz Joseph Haydn said that when he thought of God, he became so full of joy that music simply poured out of him.

Many believers find joy and express it through worship at church, but joy can permeate every aspect of life. We can give our joy away by how we live, think, and approach everything that goes on around us. For example, when we stand in a line at the grocery store, post office, or airport, we can choose not to allow the pressure of time to cloud our perspective. We can be intentional about letting our faces reflect God's joy. We can look for ways to communicate joy where we are: chatting with the people in line, looking for humor in what is going on, finding ways to help others smile, or helping someone who seems stressed by looking for evidences of God's hand in our surroundings. If none of those opportunities arises, we can pray for people we love, praise God using the alphabet as a guide, or practice any number of other holy habits.

Paul commands us in Philippians 4:4 to "rejoice in the Lord always; again I say, Rejoice!" (AMP). The exclamation mark after the second rejoice makes it a particularly emphatic instruction. Fulfilling that command — rejoicing — increases our joy. Joy is the result of:

- Believing who God is — He is a God of joy
- Letting Him live His joyful life in us — He indwells us
- Recognizing that He has united us with Himself — He has redeemed us
- Choosing to rejoice because of what He does — He fulfills His promises and gives us joy

In Numbers 6:24-26, Aaron blessed God's people by saying, "The LORD bless you and keep you; the LORD make his face shine upon you and be gracious to you; the LORD turn his face toward you and give you peace." Make that blessing your own, and bask in the pleasure of knowing that your joyful, good God, the Lord Most High, takes joy in you.

"To him who is able to keep [us] from falling and to present [us] before his glorious presence without fault and with great joy — to the only God our Savior be glory, majesty, power and authority, through Jesus Christ our Lord, before all ages, now and forevermore!" (Jude 1:24-25).

Holy Habits

- Verse to memorize: "These things have I spoken unto you, that my joy might remain in you, and that your joy might be full" (John 15:11, KJV).

- When someone smiles, take a second to thank God for making it possible for us to express joy. When you hear someone laughing, whisper a prayer of thanks for the joy reflected in the capacity for laughter. God put laughter into us, and it is part of His image.

- When you host someone (even if it is at a restaurant), intentionally make it a joyful time and thank God for His idea of hospitality.

- Make a conscious choice to thank God for the precious gift of the day He has given you. Daily commit all that will happen into His good, joyful care. Each part of the day is meant to have its own surprises. Often our lives get so busy that all we want to do is fast-forward into a period of more rest and tranquility. We may say, "When things calm down . . ." or "If only this time was over . . ." We will not welcome the gift of the day if we have already spent the emotions for living it.

- Make an appointment with God and let your body join your heart in expressing joy to Him. You could use something in creation as an impetus for you to express what you feel, such as an opening flower, a puppy, or a bird building her nest. Take time to notice the details. Choose to delight in what you see and reflect that to your heavenly Father. You may want to plan music as you give God your gift of joy.

- Start each day praying, *Lord, show me Your joyful goodness in this day.* Remind yourself of Lamentations 3:22-24: "Because of the LORD's great love we are not consumed, for his compassions never fail. *They are new every morning,* great is your faithfulness. I say to myself, 'The LORD is my portion; therefore I will wait for him'" (emphasis added). Ask Him to show you His new mercies each day.

Responding to His Word

1. Have you ever thought about God being full of joy? Why do you think it is not the first thing that comes to most people's minds when they think about God?

2. We pointed out that the opposite of joy is not sorrow. It is unbelief.[6] How did that quote impact you?

3. Read Isaiah 61:1-3,7. This passage is sometimes referred to as the mission statement of the Lord Jesus. Note the phrases that have to do with joy.

4. Isaiah's response to the significant statements in 6:1-3 and 7 is in verse 10. What does he delight in most and why?

5. In Psalm 51:16-17, what does the psalmist say that "the sacrifices of God [what He delights in]" (verse 17) are? Why would God take delight in those things?

6. Read Psalm 35:27; 37:23; Isaiah 62:4; Micah 7:18. According to

these passages, what else does God delight in?

7. Read Psalm 36:7-9. List the reasons to rejoice. What do you think the psalmist means by "your river of delights" (verse 8)? What might be included in that river?

8. What gives the psalmist joy in Psalm 16:11? How can that give you joy too?

9. Jesus says in John 15:11, "I have told you this so that my joy may be in you and that your joy may be complete." What is "this" that He refers to and how can it complete your own joy?

10. What are some of the ways you can give your joy away?

Chapter 7

Becoming One

She walked down the aisle. In her elegant wedding dress, carefully made-up, nails done, she had never felt more glamorous — or more unprepared. *What am I doing?* she wondered. During the previous weeks, she had been so caught up in wedding plans, moving, and writing thank-you notes for the myriad shower gifts that she'd had little time to think about life after the wedding. Yes, she'd looked forward to her wedding and imagined the fun of being married, but life had been too full to think about the joys and responsibilities of joining herself to the man she loved.

We do something similar in our Christian life. When we accept Christ, most of us enter the relationship like the new bride we just described. We can't possibly comprehend all that belonging to Him entails. When we marry, we gain access to facets of our husband that we did not have before: access to his body, name, and possessions. We become a part of his family, and his family becomes ours (whether we like it or not!). However, it is only as we spend time living as a married couple and as we go through the process of joining ourselves to another person that we come to understand what it means. And when we enter a relationship with God, we become a part of His body (His family) and take on His name. All that is His is available to us.

Living in the Middle of the Godhead

Learning what it means to live in the middle of the Godhead has been a transformational journey for us. Let us share with you a bit of our process. The first thing that we awakened to was a broader perspective of what it means to be in Him. God wants us to grasp the richness of being surrounded by the Godhead. John 17 is a record of the Last Supper that Jesus celebrated with His disciples, and it allows us to listen in on Jesus' prayer for all of us: "My prayer is not for them alone. I pray also for those who will believe in me through their message" (verse 20). It is clear what was on Jesus' heart for all who enter into a relationship with Him: "that all of them may be one, Father, just as you are in me and I am in you. *May they also be in us*" (verse 21, emphasis added). Even though thousands of years separate us from that event, we hear our names called: "that [Mimi and Shelly and all my children] may be one, Father, just as you are in me and I am in you. *May they also be in us.*" Jesus was praying that we would know oneness with the Godhead. Most sermons on this passage emphasize the first part of this passage, Jesus' prayer for unity among His followers. But in this chapter, we want to talk about a phrase that is often overlooked: *May they also be in us.* Did you notice the "us"? Jesus was speaking of the three-in-one nature of God. His prayer was that we would find intimacy with Him by living in the middle of who the Father, Son, and Holy Spirit are.

He also emphasizes this when He commissions His followers to "make disciples of all nations, baptizing them in the name of the Father and of the Son and of the Holy Spirit" (Matthew 28:19). The Greek word for baptize means "to immerse, submerge, to make overwhelmed."[1] According to Dallas Willard, we can understand Jesus' commission to mean that as we lead others into relationship with God, we are to lead them to being deeply immersed in the triune God.[2] We can be so totally identified with Him that we are enfolded into His nature, like a person sinking into a pool of water.

You may think, as we did, *I know I am in Christ. How is living in the Trinity any different?* This is the central question of this chapter. To answer it, we'll first need to clear away some misconceptions. As with all heavenly mysteries, we will never completely understand the Godhead. How can God be three and yet one? God has revealed enough to awaken in us a desire to know Him at a deep level, while at the same time we are aware of the unexplainable. We will need the Spirit Himself to help us. First John 2:27 tells us that the Holy Spirit "teaches you about all things." His work in the believer is like a pair of glasses for someone with bad eyesight. Without His help, we cannot see the Godhead.

The Three in One

If you ever attended Sunday school, you probably heard a variety of attempts to explain the Trinity. Teachers used examples of things that are one as a whole but have three separate parts, such as an egg. An egg has a shell, a yolk, and the white. Some used the three forms of water to help us visualize the Three in One: liquid, steam, and ice. Or they talked about how a woman is one but at the same time can be a wife, a daughter, and a mother. The problem with illustrations is that they can never fully explain the concept and they break down in the process. If we try to understand the Trinity based on human examples, we limit God.

This is because many illustrations for the Godhead focus on the *functions* of Father, Son, and Holy Spirit. That emphasis leaves out the most significant part of who the Godhead *is*. It's like trying to explain motherhood by listing what a mother does. The weakness of that approach is that a description of her function doesn't show the depth of love and commitment that is the core of who a mother is. Similarly, if we look at only the function of the Trinity, we will miss the mystery of the relationship of love that has existed among the Three in One before time.

Neither can we understand the Trinity by focusing solely on the roles of each member. They are fully and equally interconnected. The Trinity is not a hierarchy with God the Father as the Chief Executive Officer who runs everything, Jesus as the Chief Financial Officer (He paid for sin), and the Holy Spirit as the Chief Operating Officer. They do not divide their labor. They work together, breathing through one another. Jesus said, "I am in the Father and the Father is in me" (John 14:11). It is important for us to think about the relationship within the Trinity because that intimacy is what God wants us to enjoy in Him.

God — the Giver — was in eternity, and until there was a human expression of who He was, we could not enjoy a close relationship with Him. Then the Word — the Gift — became flesh and lived among us (see John 1:14). Because God clothed His heart with flesh, we can get a better look at it. We can know the heart of the Father because of the gift of His Son. Then the Son sent the Holy Spirit — the Given One — who lives in us today. The first time we see the Spirit is in Creation, where He is hovering. This is the same concept as a hen hovering over her chicks. It is a gentle attentiveness, a readiness to meet any need for nurturing. He will do His work without hurting us. He is as gentle as He was with Mary when He placed the life of Jesus in her. Through the Spirit, we enjoy the relationship God wants us to have with Him. His presence in us makes that possible. "When we receive the life of Christ through the Holy Spirit He unites us with God so that His love is demonstrated in us. The goal of the indwelling Holy Spirit is not just to unite us with God but to do it in such a way that we will be one with the Father in exactly the same way Jesus was."[3] The Bible describes it this way: "In him you too are being built together to become a dwelling in which God lives by his Spirit" (Ephesians 2:22).

The Relationship in the Three in One

Mimi learned a valuable lesson about the oneness of the Trinity when she was a little girl that starts to address the question of how living in the Trinity makes a difference.

Mimi:

I often wondered if there was a particular member of the Trinity to whom I should address my prayers because I didn't want to displease God. When I shared my concerns with a godly older man, he told me something I will never forget. He said in his deep Scottish brogue, "There is no jealousy in the Godhead." What a relief it was for me to know that when I pray to one, I pray to them all. If I pray to the Father, the Son and the Spirit take pleasure that I am drawing near. If I pray to the Son, the Father and the Spirit rejoice. If I pray to the Spirit, the same is true of the Father and the Son. Regardless which of the Three in One I address, it is God who hears my prayer.

The triune God is joy equally enjoyed and experienced in all three. Each member of the Godhead rejoices in the others. They each honor the others. Jesus often spoke of the Father receiving glory. When Jesus was baptized in the Jordan River, God the Father proclaimed the Godhead's pleasure in the Son, and God the Holy Spirit endorsed it in the form of a dove. "Because God is other oriented and is completely secure in Himself, each of the persons of the Trinity is also, and each is able to identify fully with the experiences of the others."[4]

We've talked with lots of people who either deeply appreciate or strongly dislike William P. Young's novel *The Shack*. Regardless of how you feel about how God shows up in the book, we pray that you will be open to the insights it offers about the relationship between Father, Son, and Holy Spirit. The powerful way Young portrays the *relationship* between the Trinity fits hand-in-glove with how the two of us have come to more deeply understand the Godhead. He addresses the questions *Where did love come from if it did not exist before Creation? How could God be love if He were alone?* In the book, God says, "You do understand, that unless I had . . . someone to love — if I did not have such a relationship within myself, then would I not be capable of love at all? You would have a god who could not love."[5] Love has always been a part of God; it has always been lived out between the Father, Son, and Holy Spirit. Love is who He is in the depths of His being. The Three in One is community. The dimension of love in God's character is so powerful that it binds the Three — God the Father, God the Son, and God the Holy Spirit — so closely together that they are One. God is a family.

Mack, the main human character in *The Shack*, uses a variation of our central question when he asks God what difference it makes that He is Three in One.

> *It makes all the difference in the world! . . . I am one God and I am three persons, and each of the three is fully and entirely the one. . . . What's important is this: If I were simply One God and only One Person, then you would find yourself in this Creation without something wonderful . . . [without] love and relationship. All love and relationship is possible for you only because it already exists within Me.*[6]

Mack gets a peek into the unity within the Trinity when he notices that God the Father has scars on His wrists. God tells him, "Don't ever think that what my son chose to do didn't cost us dearly. Love always leaves a significant mark. . . . We were there *together*."[7]

When you read this, does your mind go to Jesus' cry on the cross, "My God, my God, why have you forsaken me?" (Matthew 27:46)? David asked the same question in Psalm 22:1. God did not forsake David. David *felt* godforsaken. God could not look on the sin that

Jesus carried, but the decision to take away the sins of the world was not just the Son's; it was born out of the Trinity. In some mysterious way, Jesus was alone and not alone. God cannot look on our sin, but at the same time, He unconditionally promises never to leave or forsake us (see Hebrews 13:5).

When we understand that the love and relationship that exists in the Trinity is what makes all love and relationships possible, it can help us be aware of our "we-ness" with God whenever we experience intimacy.

Becoming More "We"

As new brides, it was a novelty for us to refer to our being a couple as "we." Yet after many decades of marriage, we are still growing in our understanding of what it means to be "we" with our husbands. It will take a lifetime to comprehend the true impact of two becoming one. Similarly, our unity with the Trinity makes us "we" with Him. It is a process.

In John 17:22-23, Christ refers to the oneness between Himself and the Father and says that He wants us to "know" that same oneness. He wants us to experience the deepest relationship possible with God. Professor and theologian Darrell Johnson expresses the wonder of it: "The living God draws near to me, in such a way as to draw me near to himself, to draw me into the circle of his knowing of himself."[8] This phrase merits pondering. We catch a glimpse of what being in the "circle of his knowing" means in every act of love we experience, in every relationship we enjoy. "All our longing is longing for this intimacy. We are all wired for intimacy. All our hungers are finally hunger for this; all our thirsts are ultimately thirsts for the passionate belongingness of God."[9]

When we acknowledge and accept that we were created out of God's joy and love, we experience that feeling of belonging. "Then God said, 'Let *us* make man in *our* image, in *our* likeness'" (Genesis 1:26, emphasis added). Meister Eckhart, a Dominican priest and professor of theology born in the thirteenth century, says, "Do you want to know what goes on in the core of the Trinity? I will tell you. . . . The whole Trinity laughs and gives birth to us."[10] This fills us with delight and a sense of significance. To think that we were brought forth from the pleasure within the Trinity! Not only that, but God made us to reflect the relational aspect of His character. "God does not exist alone; and neither do we who are created in God's image."[11] This is why God tells us that "it is not good for the man to be alone" (Genesis 2:18).

The Creator made Adam and breathed eternity into his lifeless form. That gift came with the breath of the Eternal One. When sin entered the picture, we did not stop being eternal, but it meant that if we stayed in sin we would spend eternity without Him. When we accept Christ's provision for our sin, we automatically step into the Trinity, which is a relationship where we will be forever with God.

It seems inconceivable that God would want us to be with Him forever. This shows that we are not His celestial project. He does not discard us once He takes care of our sin. His plan is to enjoy our company eternally and for us to enjoy His. The gift of eternity is not just unending life but also the quality of life we will spend with a good, loving, triune God. John 17:3 tells us what eternal life is: "that they may know you [the Father], the only true God, and Jesus Christ, whom you have sent." The Greek word for *know* in this passage carries the idea of deep, intimate, personal knowledge, like sexual intercourse. For example, Adam "knew" his wife Eve (Genesis 4:1, KJV).

Our sense of intimacy with the Godhead continues to grow as we find tangible ways to see ourselves in the center of the joyful, loving relationship of the Trinity. One day as Mimi greeted her husband with an extended hug and lingering kiss, one of their toddlers pushed his way through their legs and stood between them on their feet. He wanted to be in the center of their affection. Like Cal and Mimi's little guy standing in the middle of his loving parents, we can have the joy of being in the circle of loving that is the Trinity. God opens Himself to us and calls us to "the inner fellowship of God's life"[12] — into the circle of His joyful love. What a mystery, what a wonder that He welcomes us into the middle of that place!

What does that look like? When we enter into salvation, we step into the encircling arms of the Trinity, whether we realize it or not. As we grow in understanding that we live in the Godhead, we can think of ourselves as wrapped completely in an interwoven combination of the Three. This image is a picture of the hidden reality. By focusing on these holy surroundings, we can "taste and see that the LORD is good" (Psalm 34:8). We long for you to know the wonder of the fact that even though we are fallen, frail human beings, God calls us into the center of the loving, joyful goodness of His Fatherhood, His Son-made flesh, and His indwelling Spirit.

At Home in the Godhead

The idea of living in the center of the Trinity can help us look differently at Psalm 68:6, which says, "God sets the lonely in families." We have known people who believe that this verse is a promise that God will place them in a human family. We grieve over the yearning in women's hearts for belonging. It is a deep need we all have. As human beings, we naturally look to meet our loneliness through our friends, our family, our coworkers, people at church, and others, yet how small, simple, and disappointing those human relationships can be when compared to living in the reality that we are in the family of the Three in One! What we propose here is not a theory to be believed; it is the bold truth that we can mentally and emotionally lean into, like a little girl who rests in the security of her parent's love as she faces ridicule from her schoolmates.

Consider David's closing to Psalm 23, "I will dwell in the house of the LORD forever" (verse 6). He reminds us that we are a part of God's holy family. The two of us have always thought of this as in the future. Until recently we did not live with this truth as a current reality. "Living in the house of the Lord forever" is living in the Trinity *today*. Before we understood this, it was as if we had our bags packed and never truly settled into relationship with Him. As the security of being with and in Him forever seeped into our understanding, we began to realize we could rest in who God is and our position in Him. Our souls moved in and we bedded down because we are home. This is for now and eternity. We will not move again. "We-ness" with the Trinity means that we already dwell in the "secret place of the most High" and will stay "under the shadow of the Almighty" (Psalm 91:1, KJV).

Colossians 3:3 is a New Testament picture of "dwelling in the house of the Lord forever." It tells us that our lives are hidden "with Christ in God." Think of it this way: Your life "with Christ" looks like a clear glass filled with water. Now, in your mind's eye, put that full glass that is a picture of your life with Christ into a larger clear vase and fill that with water. That represents your life "with Christ in God." If you actually try it, you will notice that the glass that pictures Christ in you is completely submerged by the water in the larger container and the predominant feature is the vase, not the small glass inside. Think about the small glass surrounded by the safety and security of the water in the clear vase. When we are in the center of Him, everything that touches us is God-filtered. Jesus knew that safety as He faced death. He declared to Pilate, "You would have no power over me if it were not given to you from above" (John 19:11).

The Trinity wants us to live our lives from *within* the circle of who He is, in Him, made full. Not only do we enjoy intimacy with our Father, Jesus our Brother, and the Holy Spirit our Counselor, but because we live in them, we also possess a connection with millions of other believers as well. We have a spiritual heritage.

Everybody seems to want to know more about where they came

from — their family heritage. We have seen detailed and lengthy research that people have done to discover the history of their bloodlines. Some have been horrified when they find criminals and scoundrels in their family tree. You might know of evil in your bloodline. There could be shameful things in your past, but your spiritual heritage supersedes any family history. You can look at life from the perspective and protection of the heritage you have through the Trinity.

God's Goodness in the Trinity

The concept of God the Father, God the Son, and God the Holy Spirit shows us His goodness on many levels. The Trinity is good because it is the origin of love itself. It demonstrates that God is not exclusive. He includes and invites us all. By revealing His Triune nature, God shows us more of who He is. If God were not good *and* Triune, we would not have an example of how to reach outside of ourselves. It is in our best interests to act outside of ourselves because if there is no love, the family dies, and if the family dies, so does the individual. The persons of the Godhead are the ultimate example of one entity seeking the best of the other.

Sexuality is the most intimate expression of loving oneness between a husband and wife. Children are the by-product of this loving relationship. Could it be that the triune God designed sexual reproduction to be experienced in marriage so that we would have to form relationships in order to survive? First John 4:7-8 tell us that if we don't love we don't know God, because He is love, He is fellowship.

His Original Design

Most of us have a number of remote controls collected in baskets, and still the big challenge for a lot of us is to figure out how to turn the television on! If we were to read the manuals that came with the various controls, the possibilities are endless. When we live in the center of the Trinity, it is as if we "read the manual," and with the Holy Spirit's guidance, we begin to grasp some of the blessings of our position in Him.

For years the two of us felt that to show our appreciation to God for salvation, we should work for Him. Our relationship with God was a functional one. After all, who would teach Sunday school? Who would help save the lost and feed the hungry? Us! But as we grew to understand the full purpose of His desire for relationship with us, with the Holy Spirit's help, we began to see that, yes, we may still teach Sunday school, but now it is out of the overflow of the fullness of living within the encircling arms of the Three in One. Each day, with His help, we find identity and significance living out of the very center of the loving, joyful relationship enjoyed by the Three in One.

Another blessing of living from within the Trinity is that we both have come to know a freedom from needing to present a false self to others, to be something we are not. The Three in One continually frees us to be more of who He created us to be. When we become one with the Trinity, it is not as if we are a chocolate chip melted in a vat of chocolate that completely loses identity. In Him, we are a mighty tree with roots sunk deep into the never-ending resources of the Godhead. Father, Son, and Holy Spirit have never lost their individuality, even after living together forever. Nor will we. He made us unique. Who would know better than the Godhead how to help us fulfill His original design?

As we live out of the intimacy of the Godhead, we have come to see ourselves as being immersed in Him, encircled by who He is, while at the same time becoming freer to be truly ourselves. We have attempted to give you a glimpse of what that looks like for us. It may look different for you. God wants to show Himself to you in the way He has tailor-made for you. Expect Him to let you see His heart, to open your understanding of the joy of living in intimacy with the triune God. Ask the Spirit of God to be your teacher, to show you how to live out the truth that you dwell in the circle of the Three in One.

Oh God, we know that You moved heaven and earth to reveal Your desire for relationship with us. Please teach us to how to respond to such passionate desire. Thank You for inviting us into the very center of who You are. Give us Your insight and woo us deeper into ways of living with You. Do not let us be content with just knowing You in our heads. We want our hearts to melt as we grasp Your ardent love. We love You deeply.

Holy Habit

- Verses to memorize: "I pray . . . that all of them may be one, Father, just as you are in me and I am in you. . . . I in them and you in me. May they be brought to complete unity to let the world know that you sent me and *have loved them even as you have loved me*" (John 17:20-21,23, emphasis added).

- Fill a small glass with water. As you look at it, remind yourself that the full glass represents your life *with Christ*. Slip the glass into a pitcher or larger glass and fill that with water. That is an example of your life immersed in the Trinity. Observe that the smaller glass becomes almost transparent in the water of the bigger glass. Keep the example in a prominent place for a few days. Every time you look at it, remind yourself that you are *in* the triune God.

- Thank God every time you see people enjoying themselves. When you notice a family having fun at a park or around a table, allow it to remind you to thank the Lord for relationship. When we experience laughter and joy with others, we can better grasp the loving bond within the Trinity.

- Write out Psalm 139:5, "You hem me in — behind and before; you have laid your hand upon me." Pray the verse daily for at least a week. Each time you pray, ask God to help you understand how He immerses you in who He is.

Responding to His Word

1. Explain how you see the Trinity and the relationship between the Three in One after reading this chapter. Does the concept of the Trinity affect your walk with God? If so, how?

2. Read John 17:3 and then read Paul's words in Philippians 3:7-10. Remember that the Greek words for knowing (verse 8) and know (verse 10) refer to intimate knowledge. If we were to follow Paul's example in Philippians 3, how would that be an answer to Jesus' prayer in John 17?

3. Read John 17:26. What do you think Jesus meant when He prayed that the love God has for Him would be in us? What would that look like in practical terms?

4. Matthew 28:19 and John 17:11 both speak of the name of God. What does being "baptized in the name" mean to you? Why do you think Jesus prayed, "Protect them by the power of your name"? How can the name of God protect you?

5. Why do you think Jesus prayed what He did in John 17:15-17? How has God kept you from the evil one? How does the idea of living from within the Trinity impact your understanding of these verses?

6. What does John 17:22-23 say is yours because of your union with the Godhead? What is the purpose of those blessings?

7. Write a short summary of what Jesus' prayer in John 17 shows us of the Father's heart.

8. Describe the heavenly family that we are invited into (see Psalm 68:6). What do you understand your role to be in it?

9. Consider Romans 8:16-17, Galatians 3:27, Colossians 2:6-7, and Colossians 3:3 in regards to the relationship God has invited us

into. Briefly summarize how the concept of living in the Trinity impacts the meaning of these passages.

10. Explain in your own words what the following quote means: "The living God draws near to me in such a way as to draw me near to himself, to draw me into the circle of his knowing of himself."[13]

Chapter 8

Trusting in His Grip

If anyone had a right to question the goodness of God, Joseph did. For years his life seemed to take one bad turn after another, despite his faithful obedience to God.

As a young boy, Joseph was his father's favorite. While this definitely brought him some perks, it also had a downside. A big one. Joseph's older brothers were jealous of him and made his life difficult. Their envy continued to grow to the point that they plotted to get rid of their younger brother, so they kidnapped Joseph, imprisoned him in a pit, and sold him into slavery. To hide what they had done, they told Jacob, their father, that Joseph had died. They even showed him Joseph's bloodstained coat of many colors as "proof" that Joseph had been killed.

Joseph ended up as a slave in Egypt, yet he managed to rise to the top of where he was. Potiphar, a powerful Egyptian, recognized that Joseph was trustworthy and put him in charge of his entire household. With Joseph in charge, Potiphar was free to do Pharaoh's business. He knew things were in Joseph's capable hands. Things took an unexpected twist when Potiphar's wife, no doubt feeling lonely and neglected because her husband spent all his time with Pharaoh, took an interest in Joseph. "Now Joseph was well-built and handsome, and after a while his master's wife took notice of Joseph and said, 'Come to bed with me!'" (Genesis 39:6-7).

Joseph could have rationalized, *My master put everything he has under my care, and he didn't specifically say that his wife was off-limits. Besides, I work hard for him and what do I get in return? Nothing! He owes me! I have needs, and I have a right to have them met. Besides, he'll never find out.* But Joseph didn't give in to temptation. Instead, he said to Potiphar's wife, "How then could I do such a wicked thing and sin against God?" (verse 9). He wasn't worried about what Potiphar would think — he was concerned about what *God* would think! Potiphar's wife was so angry at being spurned that she lied to her husband, saying that Joseph had made a pass at her. Consequently, Joseph was sentenced to prison.

How would you have felt if you had been Joseph? Have you ever done the "right" thing and obeyed God, only to be punished for it? This doesn't seem fair, does it? We like to think that if we obey God, He will protect us from evil. After all, He is sovereign, isn't He? That means He has control over everything that happens to us. If He loves us, surely that must mean He will bless us with good things, right? But Joseph's story shows us that obeying God doesn't guarantee that our lives will be easy or that no harm will come to us or those we love.

You know the rest of the story. After several years, God pulled Joseph out of prison and Pharaoh made him second in command. Eventually he was reunited with his disloyal brothers. When they finally realized who he was, they were terrified that he was going to pay them back for their horrible treatment of him. He certainly had reason to. However, we get an understanding of his inner thoughts about the painful years in slavery and prison when we read that he told them, "You intended to harm me, but God intended it for good" (Genesis 50:20). For years Joseph's life was a series of painful experiences, yet as far as we know, he never lost sight of God's sovereignty.

Webster defines sovereignty as "supreme and independent power or authority."[1] Scripture tells us that God is sovereign over everything.

- "The earth is the LORD's, and everything in it, the world, and all who live in it." (Psalm 24:1)
- "Every living soul belongs to me, the father as well as the son — both alike belong to me." (Ezekiel 18:4)
- "The Most High is sovereign over the kingdoms of men.... He does as he pleases with the powers of heaven and the peoples of the earth. No one can hold back his hand or say to him: 'What have you done?'" (Daniel 4:17,35)
- "The God who made the world and everything in it is the Lord of heaven and earth.... He is not served by human hands, as if he needed anything, because he himself gives all men life and breath and everything else. From one man he made every nation of men . . . and he determined the times set for them and the exact places where they should live." (Acts 17:24-26)

God exercises His sovereignty gently and in every aspect of what He does.

Even though it took Joseph years to see what God had been up to in allowing bad things to happen to him, he never doubted God's sovereign goodness. Joseph chose to commit his life and future to God, the Absolute Ruler, the One who had total power over his life. Living in the circle of God's goodness means learning to do the same.

Leaving Our Heartaches at His Feet

People often let their hardships drive them away from God. We hear stories all the time of people who go through hard things and blame Him. How this must hurt God's heart, for we are His treasure. Instead of allowing our heartaches to come between us and God, we can choose to let the pain push us toward Him.

Shelly:

Joseph's story became real to me during the years I struggled with infertility. I had done my best to obey God all my life, yet He was withholding from me something that I longed for: children of my own. I didn't want to become bitter or resentful; I wanted to be able to trust God even though I couldn't understand what He was doing.

As you know, the Lord miraculously provided us with a baby through adoption. Not long after our first son was born, we began to try for a second adoption. One day we learned that another possibility fell through. I called Mimi, crying. She said, "I'm going to clear my schedule and come over to pray with you. We are not getting up off our knees until we have prayed through to victory."

She came. I sobbed out to the Lord and asked Him to release me from the grief and anguish of another heartbreak. Mimi helped me push, pull, and drag my hurt to the feet of Jesus and leave it there. When we finally got up off our knees, my heart was free and light. I was able to rest in the sovereignty of God for my life, confident that our heavenly Father knows what we need (see Matthew 6:32). God gave me absolute peace.

The expression "Push, pull, and drag" shows that carrying our deep hurts to the cross is work. It is easier to offer simple disappointments to Him. But when it involves the death of a dream, something that causes an emotional wound, a personal violation, a rejection, or a hurt that reaches into the core of who we are, it is nearly impossible. We do it with our will and God's loving help, realizing that it will cause us greater agony if we hold on to it (see Hebrews 12:15; Psalm 73:21-22). But the motivation to not cause ourselves further anguish is not enough. We often feel that we have a right to hold on to the hurt. Giving that right to God and taking the pain to Him has to be a decision based on what Jesus did. He died to cover and carry all our hurt, disappointment, and grief. He stands with His pierced hand outstretched and says to us, "My beloved daughter, give it to me, I gave my blood to free you of this" (Matthew 11:28, our paraphrase).

Even with that in mind, it is still a battle because we usually don't feel like letting go. We imagine that if we do, we will lose what little control we have over the situation. That's precisely the point. When we place our wounds at Jesus' feet, we release them to Him to take charge of. This is what we believe the Bible is talking about when it refers to the sacrifice of praise, or sacrifice of thanksgiving (see Psalm 116:17). We say to Him, "This is hard for me, but I love You more than my right to hold on to this. I give it to You as my sacrifice of praise, my love gift."

Have you heard the expression "The problem with living sacrifices is that they are always crawling off the altar"? We laugh at that, but the reality is that we usually take them off. When life gets tough and new pain touches us, we take back our sacrifice of praise and review the anguish. We go over what was said or done that hurt so much. That is like giving a gift and then demanding its return! We wouldn't think of doing that with a friend.

When the two of us are tempted to take back what we have placed at the foot of the cross, in our imaginations, we sink to our knees and wrap our arms around the cross. We cling to Jesus. That's where we have to live, close to Him, like Mary sitting at His feet, if we are going to be able to leave our grief with Him. What enables us to give our sacrifices of thanksgiving to Jesus is looking to Him, drawing on His love, and growing our trust in Him.

Growing Our Trust

We cannot trust God if we don't know that He is good and worthy of our trust. One way we get to know Him is by paying attention to the many names and characteristics of God in the Bible. Proverbs 18:10

tells us, "The name of the LORD is a strong tower; the righteous run to it and are safe."

Let's take a look at some of God's names and characteristics:

- **He is the defender of the defenseless, the helper of the fatherless:** "You, O God, do see trouble and grief; you consider it to take it in hand. The victim commits himself to you; you are the helper of the fatherless" (Psalm 10:14).
- **He wipes away our tears:** "God will wipe away every tear from their eyes" (Revelation 7:17).
- **He is a God of comfort:** "The God of all comfort, who comforts us in all our troubles, so that we can comfort those in any trouble with the comfort we ourselves have received from God" (2 Corinthians 1:3-4).
- **He holds us in His everlasting arms:** "The eternal God is your refuge, and underneath are the everlasting arms" (Deuteronomy 33:27).
- **He sustains and rescues us:** "Even to your old age and gray hairs I am he, I am he who will sustain you. I have made you and I will carry you; I will sustain you and I will rescue you" (Isaiah 46:4).

Shelly learned firsthand how standing on the names of God can help us trust God when our circumstances fill us with fear.

Shelly:

When we moved back to the States, we had to send our boys to a large public school. They had always gone to Christian schools and been around people we knew. It was difficult for me to trust in God's sovereign goodness in this new situation. The first day I dropped Carl off at his new high school, I was terrified. What have we done? Everything the world has to offer is available to him here! We have

loved and protected him, and now we've just opened the door to the
lion's den. Fear made my chest ache, and tears streamed down my
cheeks.

As I returned to our new home, I practiced the holy habit of
asking, "Lord, who are You in this situation?" His name, "The God
who Sees" (see Genesis 16:13-14), came to mind. I prayed, "Lord,
You are the God who sees Carl when I can't. I choose to trust You
to watch over him." I also remembered that He is, "The God who
is There" (see Ezekiel 48:35) when I can't be. "Lord, You are there
with Carl," I declared by faith. I imagined God not only seeing our
son but also being right with him in the crowded hallways. By the
time I got home, my fears were under control because I had chosen to
believe the promise of God's presence with Carl. "The peace of God,
which transcends all understanding" (Philippians 4:7) guarded my
emotions and my thinking the rest of the day. The next day the fear
came back and I had to start all over again.

Scripture is also full of promises that assure us that we can trust
that God is acting in goodness no matter what He allows in our lives
or in the lives of those we love. Here are just a few truths we can stand
on when circumstances might cause us to doubt God's goodness.

- **God has a plan for your life, and that plan is to give you a**
  hope-filled future. "'I know the plans I have for you,' declares
  the LORD, 'plans to prosper you and not to harm you, plans to
  give you hope and a future'" (Jeremiah 29:11).
- **God is near when you suffer.** "The LORD is close to the
  brokenhearted and saves those who are crushed in spirit"
  (Psalm 34:18).
- **He uses everything in your life to make you like Himself.**
  "We know that in all things God works for the good of
  those who love him, who have been called according to

his purpose . . . to be conformed to the likeness of his Son" (Romans 8:28-29).

- **Your pain is not wasted.** "Our . . . troubles are achieving for us an eternal glory that far outweighs them all" (2 Corinthians 4:17).
- **One day, with Him, the pain and suffering will all be gone.** "There will be no more death or mourning or crying or pain, for the old order of things has passed away" (Revelation 21:4).
- God's **actions** also demonstrate His sovereign goodness.

"The Sovereign LORD *comes* with power. . . . He *tends* his flock like a shepherd: He *gathers* the lambs in his arms and *carries* them close to his heart; he gently *leads* those that have young" (Isaiah 40:10-11, emphasis added).

"In him we have *redemption* through his blood, the *forgiveness* of sins, in accordance with the riches of God's *grace* that he *lavished* on us with all wisdom and understanding" (Ephesians 1:7-8, emphasis added).

"He who *began* a *good work* in you will *carry* it on *to completion*" (Philippians 1:6, emphasis added).

"*Great and marvelous are your deeds*, Lord God Almighty. Just and true are your ways, King of the ages" (Revelation 15:3, emphasis added).

We cannot separate God's sovereignty from His goodness. Everything He does flows out of who He is; everything He does confirms His sovereign goodness. His sovereignty and His goodness are the foundation we can stand on when things around us are falling apart. We can have hope.

The Doorway to Hope

We can see the Rocky Mountains from our windows. When we go hiking, we often see rock climbers. They hammer pitons — spikes — into tiny cracks in the cliffs, attach ropes through them, and climb sheer rock faces. When we choose to trust in God's sovereign goodness, it's as if we are driving a piton into the rock of His character. As He proves Himself trustworthy, it helps us trust Him in the midst of even greater challenges. Oswald Chambers wrote, "Faith is not some weak and pitiful emotion, but is strong and vigorous confidence. . . . Faith is the supreme effort of your life — throwing yourself with abandon and total confidence upon God."[2]

When we pound a piton into the rock of God's character, hope replaces fear. Paul and Timothy had every human reason to be resentful toward God. "We do not want you to be uninformed . . . about the hardships we suffered in the province of Asia. We were under great pressure, far beyond our ability to endure, so that we despaired even of life" (2 Corinthians 1:8). These men had given their lives to God, and it seemed that all they got for it was trouble. Not only did they think they could not endure the difficult circumstances they were facing, they weren't sure they were going to live.

Scripture does not tell us what perils Paul was referring to. However, we do know how he and Timothy responded to their difficulties: "Indeed, in our hearts we felt the sentence of death. But this happened that we might not rely on ourselves but on God, who raises the dead" (verse 9). They knew they worshipped a God so powerful that He could raise the dead.

Second Corinthians goes on to tell us what Paul and Timothy learned because they took a firm position on God's sovereignty in the midst of deep challenges. "He has delivered us from such a deadly peril, and he will deliver us. On him we have set our hope that he will continue to deliver us" (verse 10). God's faithfulness was a hook they could hang their trust on for the next trial. We can hang our trust too. We can also encourage one another to hope in God.

Helping Each Other Trust

Paul ends his description of what he and Timothy learned in Asia with a curious statement: "as you help us by your prayers" (2 Corinthians 1:11). How interesting that this great man of God, who probably had more to do with the spread of Christianity than any other single individual, acknowledged his need for the prayers of others. We can help people who are facing difficult situations trust His sovereign grip on their lives by reminding them of who He is, what His promises are, and what He does.

The two of us sometimes receive calls from women who are desperate. After hearing their anguish and acknowledging the weight of their burdens, we pray with them, reminding ourselves and them of the character of God, and then worship Him for His sovereignty in their situation. Sometimes we say to a particularly weary person who wants to trust but is struggling, "We will believe for you and talk to God on your behalf." We are putting a piton into the rock of His character. We assure them that God, in His sovereign goodness, sees the big picture. He has a God's-eye view.

When we trust in God's good sovereignty, we choose to believe He is Lord over all and that nothing catches Him by surprise. When we are sure of His sovereignty, it does three things: lifts our anxiety, releases us from having to understand the whys of our challenges, and helps us place our pain in His hands. It reminds us that although we have no control over what happens to us, God does and He is good.

You can't know what will happen in the next hour, day, week, month, or year, but you can trust in the sovereign Master and Lord, who is already there.

Sovereign Lord, help us stand on who You are for our challenges today. Help us not to forget that You know the beginning from the end, You have all power, and You want to work on our behalf. As we know You more, may our hope in You grow ever stronger. Thank You that You make the areas of our fear, sin, hurt, and disappointment into a door of hope. We love You.

Holy Habits

- Verses to memorize: "Praise be to the name of God for ever and ever; wisdom and power are his. He changes times and seasons; he sets up kings and deposes them. He gives wisdom to the wise and knowledge to the discerning. He reveals deep and hidden things; he knows what lies in darkness, and light dwells with him" (Daniel 2:20-22).

- One sign of trust in God's sovereignty is thankfulness. Spend a few minutes each day thanking God, starting with thanking Him for making you the way He did, for different parts of your body. Move on to thanking Him for the circumstances in your life. Work on choosing to thank God for being in control of your life, even for those things that don't make sense.

- When you are facing a difficulty, cultivate the holy habit of asking God, "Who are You in this situation?" If you need to be reminded of His names and characteristics, go to the Psalms. Choose several (some of our favorites are 145, 146, and 147) and make a list of what you find there. It's a powerful exercise just to read these names and be reminded of *who* it is that you walk with.

- Remind yourself of what God has done for you. To help you maintain a God's-eye view, keep a miracle book, or journal, in which you list the ways God proves Himself trustworthy and faithful to you. Review them often.

Responding to His Word

1. Look up the following verses about God's sovereignty: Isaiah 8:13; Acts 4:24; Luke 2:29; 1 Timothy 6:15; 1 Peter 3:15; Revelation 6:10. Even if your translation does not use the words sovereign or sovereignty, how do you see it in these passages?

2. Why is His sovereignty significant in the verses mentioned in question 1?

3. Read Matthew 6:25-33. What do these verses mean to you in light of God's sovereignty? How does thinking about this passage through the filter of God's sovereignty change your understanding of it?

4. Read the following passages: 1 Samuel 15:29; Psalm 33:11; Isaiah 26:4; Hebrews 6:17-18; James 1:17. Why is God's unchanging nature an important part of His sovereignty? What can it mean for you in your everyday life?

5. Read Romans 1:28-32. From these verses, why do you think it is so important to recognize and thank God for His sovereign work?

6. How can the names and characteristics of God help you get a broader picture of His sovereignty?

7. Read 2 Corinthians 1:8-11 to find out what Paul and Timothy went through. Why did they believe that God allowed the experience?

8. How might Paul and Timothy's approach to their circumstances be an example to you in dealing with hard times? What has God done that you could use as pitons in order to trust Him for the future?

9. How can God's sovereignty give you hope?
10. Write a prayer of thanks for God's sovereignty in your life.

Chapter 9

Beyond "Till Death Do Us Part"

A winter storm watch was posted for the entire state of North Dakota. Everyone was rushing home to beat the storm. Cheryl sat huddled in a heavy wool coat, waiting for her car to warm up. Her briefcase was packed with paperwork to help her get through the lonely, cold hours that lay ahead. On the way home, she stopped at the grocery store, which was packed. There was excitement in the air as kids shopping with their mothers anticipated a few days of sledding, ice skating, and other joys of a snowstorm. A familiar dark cloud descended on Cheryl's heart. How she longed for someone to share the winter with her, for someone to snuggle with while the wind howled outside her windows!

Cheryl was just a little girl when her father set off to find his fortune in the oil fields of the Middle East. It was not long before he sent word that he wasn't coming home. Her mom found work in a nearby nursing home. They were short-staffed and she worked overtime. Her mother then started a relationship with a man from work, and she left Cheryl on her own for long hours. As her mother took less and less time to be with her, Cheryl felt abandoned by both her mother and her father. She spent that time reading, fleeing her lonely world into the exciting realm of fairy tales, mysteries, and romances. Her childhood escape grew into adult fantasy, and soon the romantic novels she lived in occupied her heart and her thoughts. All she wanted was someone who would love her and enjoy her company. She had so much to give to a relationship, but the opportunity to express that desire never came. As the years went by, her dream of belonging seemed to be hopeless. Mechanically, she turned away from the lively buzz at the grocery store to face another storm, another winter, another year alone.

Though the details may be different, Cheryl's sad, painful story is all too familiar. We all want to belong to someone, to know that we can feel "safe" and loved. What hope is there for us when we feel rejected and abandoned by the people who are supposed to be there for us? Is there no one who will make a lifelong commitment, to whom we can safely belong?

We've discovered the answer is yes. God offers that hope.

Some of you are probably thinking, *I've heard that before. What's new?* If that's you, don't put the book down. Stick with us for a few more pages.

The Only One Who Will Always Be Faithful

There is wonderful, life-changing hope. God offers an unbreakable covenant to Cheryl and to us. According to *Strong's Exhaustive Concordance*, "God's 'covenant' is a relationship of love and loyalty."[1] It goes beyond anything we can comprehend. The word *covenant* carries the idea of a deep, sacred, and unbreakable promise or oath. In Scripture, God's covenant is a pledge that "refers to the act of God in freely establishing a mutually binding relationship with humankind."[2] He offers relationship to us and does not withdraw it, even though we might feel rejected and abandoned.

What is the promise of this God-made covenant? Simply put, every covenant God has made with humankind is about relationship. God promises union with Himself, and He backs up the promise with His covenant. He offers us the opportunity to find our home with Him.

The theme of God's sacred oaths to His people runs throughout Scripture:

- **God's covenant is eternal.** "I will establish my covenant as an everlasting covenant between me and you and your descendants after you for the generations to come, to be your God and the God of your descendants after you" (Genesis 17:7).
- **God's covenant is secure.** "Has [God] not made with me an everlasting covenant, arranged and secured in every part?" (2 Samuel 23:5).
- **God's covenant is love.** "Know therefore that the LORD your God is God; he is the faithful God, keeping his covenant of love to a thousand generations" (Deuteronomy 7:9).
- **God's covenant cannot be shaken.** "Though the mountains be shaken and the hills be removed, yet my unfailing love for you will not be shaken nor my covenant of peace be removed" (Isaiah 54:10).
- **God's covenant is sealed by the blood of Jesus.** "This is my blood of the covenant, which is poured out for many for the forgiveness of sins" (Matthew 26:28).
- **God's covenant is written in our hearts.** "This is the covenant I will make . . . declares the Lord. I will put my laws in their minds and write them on their hearts. I will be their God, and they will be my people" (Hebrews 8:10).

The Old Testament speaks of God's firm commitment to union with the Israelites, His chosen ones. The New Testament introduces an even greater covenant made through Jesus Christ and offered to all humanity. God did not erase the first contract; He expanded it. "The New Covenant is far superior to the Old Covenant in that it affords true forgiveness and cleansing from sin. There is no covering (atonement) for sin under the New Covenant. There is no need for one.

The sin question was settled at Calvary.... The Messiah did away with our atonement."[3] Jesus' once-and-for-all sacrifice permanently ended the need for the atonement, or animal sacrifices. Jesus' death opened the door for a deeper level of relationship than Old Testament believers could have imagined.

The modern-day example of the credit card might help us better understand the difference between the Old and New Covenants. "A credit card has no intrinsic value.... But it is accepted in lieu of cash ... because it is a forerunner ... of the true payment which is to follow. Until that time, the credit card covers the purchase."[4] The Old Covenant was a shadow of the new, greater one that came with Christ's death. The "credit card" or repeated animal sacrifices are not necessary because Jesus backs the New Covenant with His blood, which paid for all our past debt and our future debt too. In other words, the life of His Son stands behind God's offer to us of intimate relationship.

A vivid Middle Eastern allegory in Ezekiel 16 paints a powerful picture of how even under the Old Covenant, God stepped in to address the rejection and abandonment of a newborn girl. Many of us can identify with the feelings of rejection and abandonment in this passage, even though our circumstances may be different.

> On the day you were born your cord was not cut, nor were you washed with water to make you clean, nor were you rubbed with salt or wrapped in cloths. No one looked on you with pity or had compassion.... Rather, you were thrown out into the open field, for on the day you were born you were despised.
>
> Then I passed by and saw you kicking about in your blood, and as you lay there in your blood I said to you, "Live!" (verses 4-6)

In this allegory, God rescued the discarded baby girl and watched over her as she grew up. When she was ready and able to respond to His love, He offered her a relationship with Himself (see verse 8), a belonging she had never known. She had nothing to give God in return, yet He chose to extend His care over her. "He set His love on her" (see Deuteronomy 10:15) because He wanted to. Theologians call that *grace*, which means favor she did not deserve.

The God who cared about the rejected child in Ezekiel also turns His face toward Cheryl and toward us. He sees our need to belong. God is the pursuer, the One who takes the initiative to draw us and offer a union with Him. In this allegory, He announced, "I gave you my solemn oath and entered into a covenant with you . . . and you became mine" (16:8). God made a covenant with the abandoned girl even though He knew she had nothing to give Him but herself.

As the allegory unfolds, we begin to see the reasons for God's tender care for her and for us. It would be enough that He rescues us from sure spiritual death, but He wants to do something so much deeper; He wants to make us His bride. This is not out of a personal need He has. God does not need anything or anyone to be complete. We are satisfied in our earthly relationships only if the other people meet our needs. God gives Himself to us because He wants us. He *longs for* relationship with you. Need does not motivate Him. He reaches out to you simply because He desires the very best for you.

What He Does for Us

God's covenant — His promise of relationship — is eternal, secure, loving, sealed by Jesus' blood, and forever written on our hearts. God confirmed His covenant in the story in Ezekiel with gifts that He showered on the girl. He provided soft leather sandals to protect her feet from the burning desert sands. He gave her garments of fine linen and silk (see Ezekiel 16:10). He spared no expense to provide beauty for His bride. He beautified her arms, neck, nose, ears, and head with gold. The gracious Lover says, "I adorned you with jewelry" (verse 11). Not only did He rescue her, He chose her to be His precious bride.

Mimi:

When I read this allegory, it reminds me of the time I stood in a Middle Eastern gold market watching a young girl and her parents examine the gold jewelry that would be her dowry. In such a culture, the gold a bride brings into marriage provides her with financial security in case her husband dies or leaves her. I attended a wedding where the bride stood before her groom while he ceremoniously draped her with jewelry from a tray full of gold.

Our girl in Ezekiel had no parents to provide her dowry, so her heavenly bridegroom provided her with gold, and security, from His own treasure. Concerned with more than providing beautiful things for her outward needs, God, the attuned Lover, continued to affirm His covenant by attending to her bodily needs as well. He washed her and put fragrance on her (see Ezekiel 16:9). He fed her with the best food (see verse 13). God made an unshakeable commitment to her. He was her supreme Protector, her Provider, and her Lover. She could bask in the wonder of His favor resting on her. He did everything to capture her heart.

He does the same with us. God confirms His desire for relationship with us through a variety of gifts. Much of what He provides is internal confirmation of the spiritual reality that we enjoy in our union with Him.

What gifts does God give us because of His good, eternal covenant?

- He etches the truth of His commitment to us on our hearts and minds (see Hebrews 8:10). This is the work of God's Holy Spirit.
- The clothing He gives us is the splendor of Jesus Christ Himself (see Romans 13:14). Who Jesus is and what His death did for us covers our otherwise naked hearts.

- The gold He gives us is the invaluable gift of our life tried and purified under His loving protection (see Job 23:10).
- The jewelry is a crown of life, love, and compassion (see James 1:12; Psalm 103:4). When we think of this "crown," which is far lovelier than any that the Queen of England owns, it makes us hold our heads higher.
- He nourishes us with His Word (see Psalm 119:103).
- He satisfies our spiritual hunger and thirst (see Psalm 107:9).
- He gives us good things (see Psalm 84:11). He provides not only spiritual gifts but also tangible things such as sunshine and rain, flowers and trees, and at the same time furnishes us with spiritual blessings that are good for our souls. There is the goodness of a hearty laugh, a quiet space to think, and heart connection with Him.

Second Chronicles 16:9 tells us another thing God does for us when we are in a covenant relationship with Him: "The eyes of the LORD run to and fro throughout the whole earth, to show Himself strong on behalf of those whose heart is loyal [fully committed] to Him" (NKJV). God does not passively sit in heaven. No, His eyes run all over the earth on our behalf! The Scriptures tell us that Satan walks around the earth (see Job 1:7), but God *runs*. He gets there first! He hurries to strengthen us when we are His. The list of things God makes available to us because of His covenant is endless.

Whether or not we choose to enjoy a covenant relationship with God, everything good that we have is a loving gift from Him. Most of us didn't realize it at the time, but when we asked Jesus into our lives to be Lord, we accepted His covenant. However, most believers don't comprehend the implications of the depth of commitment God makes to us. It is as if when we accept Christ, we enter a new home but choose to live in the entry by the front door. To fully enjoy the profound relationship God offers us through His covenant, we need to go further in.

We must figuratively take off our shoes, go into the family room, curl up on the couch, and allow ourselves to be safe and at home in order to truly belong. Our good, covenant-making God makes all He is available to us when we choose to enter into union with Him.

Our Part?

Have you ever wondered why God doesn't force us into relationship with Him? After all, He's sovereign — He can do what He wants. Why would He go through the process of wooing us and then allow us to choose whether or not to unite ourselves with Him? One simple answer is that He loves to be the pursuer, the initiator. He loves to love. Each day, because He is good, He plans to show us more of Himself, if we will notice. Another reason is that He is more honored when we choose Him than if we had no choice. In His goodness, He never insists that anyone have a relationship with Him against his or her will. He delights in our choice to love Him, and He is willing to wait for it.

God wants our heart — our whole heart — as well as our mind and soul and strength. We can choose to accept or reject Him. Multiple times the Israelites vowed to do "everything the LORD has said" (Exodus 19:8), but within weeks they forgot their sacred trust and sought after lesser gods. If it were up to us to be faithful to God and keep His ways, we too could not do it. The Israelites' breaking of their part of the Old Testament covenant is proof that even if we wanted to fulfill our part of the bargain, goodwill could never do it. We would fail without the help of God's Holy Spirit. When we choose to join in deep union with Him, the Spirit of God daily teaches us how to live.

What keeps us from that life? Why do we question the covenant God offers to us? Why is it hard to accept the truth of it?

Lies We Believe

If you read the rest of the story in Ezekiel 16, you'll see that the young woman, who represents the nation of Israel, didn't trust God's promise and the covenant He so lovingly offered her. We wonder if she prostituted herself and spent the gifts God gave her, trying to earn human affection, because she never really believed God's commitment to her. She looked everywhere else to prove she didn't deserve rejection.

We do the same. Many of us may be able to believe enough to accept His offering of salvation but don't dare go any deeper because of what we fear it might cost us. Or we struggle to trust that God will keep His commitment to us, since everybody else in our lives has failed. Examples of unbroken faithfulness are few. Events of broken trust and rejection open up gaping wounds in our spirit, and we can feel them hemorrhaging out of the deep pain we carry.

Satan, God's enemy, speaks lies that fall into the fertile ground of our pain and our wounds. *There it is again*, he whispers. *You can't trust anybody. All you ever get is rejection and hurt. No one cares enough about you to love you unconditionally, to want to have you around.* The lies take immediate root and begin to dominate our lives.

Satan and his henchmen are so astute that they hook more lies into the wound that is so tender and susceptible to further hurt. Soon the lies become a part of the way we think. Once we believe them, we act on them. Cheryl's wound first opened when she was a little girl and her father walked out of her life. The lie that was whispered into her pain was that no one cared enough to be committed to her. Pastor Steve Holt says, "Satan and his demons script our thinking at an early age."[5] Cheryl's wound deepened and the lie was reinforced by her mother's emotional and physical absence. The repeated disappointments in her romantic relationships caused it to become a cancerous conviction.

Even though Cheryl is a Christian and knows about God's commitment to her, she did not understand that the union He offers her can heal her wounds and meet her deepest needs on a human level. First John 3:8 announces, "The reason the Son of God appeared was to destroy the devil's work." The word *destroy* means to replace, undo, loosen, or dissolve.

The Healing Truth

How can God's covenant — His unbreakable promise of relationship — undo or dissolve the deep wound in our hearts? When we combat a lie, our natural instinct is to think that the opposite is the truth. But in Cheryl's case, the opposite of the lie that nobody could keep a commitment to her was still a lie! The opposite of the lie was that some person *would* come through, and we know that no human can perfectly fulfill a commitment. So if the opposite of the lie is not the answer, what's the healing truth?

The healing truth is always something about the character of God and what that truth makes us because of our union with Him. For Cheryl, the healing truth is based on what God offers her: an eternal, unbreakable covenant relationship that goes way beyond "till death do us part." Regardless of whether another human being is ever faithful to her, because of her union with God, Cheryl is beloved by the King of kings and the Lord of lords. He calls her His very own! (see Song of Songs 6:3; 1 Timothy 6:15; 1 Samuel 12:22). He backs His good covenant with His unfailing character and the precious blood of His only Son.

In order to combat the lies of rejection and abandonment, Cheryl had to learn to apply the healing truth. She needed to identify the wounds and the lies that Satan had planted into her pain. One of Cheryl's wounds was her father's abandonment of her and her mother. By the time her mother gave up pretending to care for Cheryl, the lie that she was worthy of abandonment was firmly rooted. Satan whispered to her, "Everybody will reject you." Broken dating relationships reinforced that lie and confirmed another one that had been trying to make its way into her heart: "Nobody will ever really love you." Other lies she believed included "There must be something wrong with you because everybody leaves," "You are a bad person because no one wants you," "If you work really hard, you can make people love you," and on and on.

The next step was to take those lies to God and pray, *Father, I have believed the following lies that have been whispered into my heart.* (Name each one of the lies.) *In the name of Jesus Christ and by the blood shed on Calvary, I break the power of those lies. Through the victory won by the death and resurrection of Jesus Christ, I stand against the evil forces that want me to live in the wounding.*

Then Cheryl needed to ask God to help her find Scriptures that affirmed the healing truth. We often recommend that women personalize Ephesians 1:3-14, reading it aloud and replacing "us," "we," and "you" with their own name.

> *Praise be to the God and Father of our Lord Jesus Christ, who has blessed _____ in the heavenly realms with every spiritual blessing in Christ. For he chose _____ in him before the creation of the world to be holy and blameless in his sight. In love he predestined _____ to be adopted as his [daughter] through Jesus Christ, in accordance with his pleasure and will—to the praise of his glorious grace, which he has freely given _____ in the One he loves. In him _____ [has] redemption through his blood, the forgiveness of sins, in accordance with the riches of God's grace that he lavished on _____ with all wisdom and understanding. And he made known to _____ the mystery of his will according to his good pleasure, which he purposed in Christ.... In him _____ [was] also chosen, having been predestined according to the plan of him who works out everything in conformity with the purpose of his will,*

in order that _____ . . . might be for the praise of his glory.
And _____ also [was] included in Christ when [she] heard
the word of truth, the gospel of [her] salvation. Having believed,
_____ [was] marked in him with a seal, the promised
Holy Spirit, who is a deposit guaranteeing _____'s inherit-
ance. . . . To the praise of his glory.

Revelation 12:11 talks about how to combat the accuser: "They overcame him by the blood of the Lamb and by the word of their testimony." We have tremendous power against the Enemy when we audibly declare the truth.

Cheryl learned that applying the healing truth did not mean denying her grief and pain. Instead, it meant acknowledging it before God. She learned to offer up her feelings to Him: *Lord, I am deeply hurt. I ache over my father leaving when I was so young, over my mother choosing a man over her own daughter. I want so badly to erase the lonely ugliness of the past years. I am mad at my father and my mother. I give what I'm feeling to You. I pour it out before You.* She came to understand that she could choose to take each painful thought to God, over and over again. Then she could declare these healing truths:

- "In love He predestined *me*, Cheryl, to be adopted as His daughter in accordance with His pleasure and will" (see Ephesians 1:5).
- "The riches of God's grace have been lavished on *me*" (see Ephesians 1:7).
- "He chose *me* to love before the foundation of the earth!" (see Ephesians 1:4).

If we permit it, the healing truth can transform us one thought, one moment, at a time. God does not get tired of us repeating ourselves. He wants us to tell Him, even if it is for the thousandth time, what hurts.

Then as we declare His truth over those wounds and lies, He heals us and we become more and more sure of the unwavering covenant He makes to us.

The Choice Before You

God wants us to let Him address the painful messages from our past. He says, "Listen, beloved, pay attention. Take this to heart. Put the pain and wounds of your past behind you. I am the King, and everything about you pleases Me. Make Me your first priority. Let Me be in charge" (Psalm 45:10-11, our paraphrase). We honor our good, covenant-making God by letting Him redeem our past and keeping our love commitment to Him. That makes us better wives, mothers, friends, aunts, neighbors, and citizens because we interact with others out of the assurance that we belong to the King of kings and Lord of lords. We look to Him for security, and that allows us to relieve everyone else of the pressure of providing it for us.

During his final discourse to the Israelites, Moses says to the people of the covenant,

> *This day I call heaven and earth as witnesses against you that I have set before you life and death, blessings and curses. Now choose life, so that you and your children may live and that you may love the LORD your God, listen to his voice, and hold fast to him. For the LORD is your life. (Deuteronomy 30:19-20)*

The principles in this verse are pivotal for standing on the truth. Before each of us is the choice between life and death, blessings and curses. Life and blessings come from the healing truth; death and curses come from the wounds and lies. We see so many women living in the Enemy's camp, unaware that death and curses are a result of their choices. All of us choose where we are going to live. What are you letting yourself believe? What is your self-talk? Is it full of life messages or death messages?

God Most High offers you a glorious relationship. He gave you life and sustained it until you were old enough to accept His love and participate with Him in a covenant relationship. With the tenderness that only a good God can express, He woos you to Himself and offers you an eternal commitment. Satan doesn't want you to believe that God can heal your wounds. When you accept His covenant, you can apply the healing truth and say, "I am Yours, and You are mine." Even when He has won your heart, He does not stop. He continues to woo you. You can find your security and assurance in God's covenant as you understand His deep unshakeable commitment and love for you.

Lord, we are awed that You would choose to make an unbreakable promise to us. Thank You for Your good, loving covenant. Reveal to us the lies that keep us from grasping the depth of Your commitment to us. Teach us Your healing truth for our pain so we can choose life and blessings. Help us to never lose sight of You.

Holy Habits

- Verses to memorize: "If you obey me fully and keep my covenant, then out of all nations you will be my treasured possession. Although the whole earth is mine, you will be for me" (Exodus 19:5-6).

- Plan a time of worship. Choose a piece of music that lifts your heart. As you listen to it, praise God. Thank Him for choosing, loving, and providing for you. Reaffirm your commitment to Him.

- Find things you can use to lift your heart in thanks to the God who chooses to make a covenant with you. For example, when you see a rainbow, either in nature or one made by sun shining through a prism, thank God for His covenant promises to you (see Genesis 9:16). We have hung prisms in our windows so we can see rainbows every day.

- Write out the healing truth for the lies you believe and the wounds you carry. Repeat it aloud every morning as you wash your face and brush your teeth. Throughout the day, combat the thoughts Satan uses to try to defeat you, one at a time, by declaring again the healing truth.

Responding to His Word

1. God chose us without our deserving it. It is pure grace. Study Romans 5:15-17; 2 Corinthians 9:8-9; Ephesians 1:7-8. What do these verses tell you about the grace God extends to you?

2. The allegory in Ezekiel 16 shows God washing and cleansing the girl. Study the following verses: 1 Corinthians 6:11; Ephesians 5:25-26; Hebrews 9:14; Revelation 7:14. According to these verses, how does He cleanse us?

3. Marriage is a covenant relationship. What parallels do you see between marriage and a commitment to God?

4. The theme of God's covenant with us runs throughout Scripture. What does His covenant teach you about God?

5. Read Deuteronomy 10:15; Isaiah 41:9-10; John 15:16; Colossians 3:1; 1 Peter 1:2. According to these passages, what is God's purpose in choosing you for relationship? What (if any) response do the verses say is required of you?

6. What do you feel about having a choice to respond to God's covenant?

7. Jesus tells us in Mark 12:30 how we are to love God. Why do you think He wants you to do it in these four ways? For each facet, describe what loving Him that way would look like for you.

8. What lie or wound can you identify in your life? What is a healing truth that you can apply to that lie or wound?

9. Based on Moses' call to the Israelites in Deuteronomy 30:19-20, list three aspects of life and blessing that are before you right now.

10. See Deuteronomy 30:20. How could your answers to question 9 help you do the following?
   - Love God
   - Listen to His voice
   - Hold fast to Him

Chapter 10

Shipwrecks Turned Gorgeous Coral Reefs

Betty grew up in a Christian home with little money but lots of love. Her parents treasured her and protected her from the harsh realities of life. In high school she met Mark; she was immediately drawn to his good looks and intelligence. They became friends, but she knew her parents would not allow their relationship to be anything more because Mark was not a believer.

Mark began attending Young Life meetings just to be with Betty because she was adamant that she wouldn't date him. Soon he understood his need for a relationship with Jesus and asked Him into his heart. When Betty took him home to meet her parents, they loved him. He started going to church with her and reading his Bible; she could see he was interested in spiritual things and she let herself fall in love. It was a long courtship and they married after graduating from college.

Betty put Mark through graduate school so he could pursue his dream of becoming a university professor. He also liked working on his inventions. Even though their lives were busy, they kept closely connected and were very much in love. They had fun together and lived almost a fairy-tale romance.

In time Mark became a respected professor and inventor and he and Betty had two boys, four years apart. That's when she began to feel as though her life wasn't turning out the way she had dreamed it would. Mark was away from home for longer and longer periods of time, ostensibly because of his work. Betty had to function as a single mom and felt lonely and isolated. Still, whenever Mark was free, they went to church as a family, and she was able to convince herself that all was well.

But over time she started noticing signs that Mark was busy with more than work during his long absences from home. He was gone a lot on weekends, and he often stepped out of the room to take phone calls. Unusual charges started showing up on their credit card, and friends mentioned they had seen Mark in odd places. As evidence mounted, Betty could no longer deny that something was wrong. Seriously wrong. When she confronted him, Mark admitted to being involved in the ugly things she suspected. He was addicted to pornography and visiting prostitutes and was involved in other disturbing activities. He also told her that he had no desire or intention to stop; he didn't think he was doing anything wrong. When Mark said that, she felt as if she had died inside. It robbed her of any hope that things would get better. She thought, *How could this happen to me? All I have ever done is love my husband and try to be a good wife to him.*

For appearance's sake, they decided not to divorce. Her sons were the only reason Betty got up in the morning. She struggled valiantly to be both father and mother to their boys. She taught them well and gave them every opportunity to make wise choices, but now all that was falling apart too. They were acting out the pain from their father's emotional abandonment. Her older son was into drugs, sometimes stealing to support his habit, and the younger one was sexually active and constantly slipping out to go to wild parties. Her boys had become adults who excused their behavior because it wasn't as bad as their father's. She felt helpless. Betty wondered, *What can I do? My husband lied to me and rejected me. My sons, who were my joy, break my heart every day with their destructive choices. I am afraid where they will end up.* Betty's thoughts were torturing her, and despair gripped her spirit.

Perhaps you are reading this book because you have felt the same way Betty does. Whether through your own choices or those of the people you love, your life has not turned out as you had hoped. Like Betty you are wondering, *Will the future bring me only more pain and disappointment? Where is the abundant life that Christians are promised in John 10:10?*

When we heard Betty's story, we wanted to assure her that not only did her Creator make and redeem her but He also wanted to re-create her by using the ugly things in her life to make something lovely.

A Picture of Re-Creation

Here is a picture of what He can do.

Mimi:

Cal and I were in the Caribbean with our family for a week's vacation. Just outside our hotel window, the tip of a ship that sank more than sixty years ago punctuated the aqua waters. Fascinated with the old wreck, we scheduled a snorkeling trip to see it as soon as possible. As we snorkeled above the surface, we saw colorful coral and sea plants completely covering the old boat beneath the waterline. Schools of tropical fish, whose shimmering scales caught the filtered light from the surface, kept us spellbound. Under the water, we could barely discern the outline of the vessel; the teeming life that inhabited the old frame almost obliterated any sign of it.

Knowing that saltwater is highly corrosive, we asked our guide why we saw no evidence of decomposing metal from the wreck. He told us that no rust leached into the sea from the iron hull because of the life that covered every inch of its surface. What could have been an environmental disaster had become a tourist attraction because of the beauty covering it.

God can do the same with us. He can take the shipwrecks of our lives and turn them into beautiful coral reefs, vibrant with life. He created us, He redeemed us, and He wants to re-create us. Beth Moore says it well: "Redemption is incomplete if our negative past is only diffused. Satan won't be completely sorry and God won't get all the glory until the bad is used for good."[1] Even though the shipwreck was a disaster and the ship could no longer fulfill its original purpose, God re-created it into something beautiful.

Living in the circle of God's goodness means trusting that when our lives are derailed by our own or others' sinful choices, God wants to re-create us into something new and good. We see this in Isaiah 1:18, which says,

> *"Come now, let us reason together,"*
> *says the LORD.*
> *"Though your sins are like scarlet,*
> *they shall be as white as snow;*
> *though they are red as crimson,*
> *they shall be like wool."*

Always Part of the Plan

God created life and beauty simply by speaking them into existence. Although He could have done everything with His word, for His final act He leaned over and "formed" humankind from the ground. The raw material was mud. God breathed life into the inanimate mud form. This was His first personal interaction with us. He chose to make us and to bless us with His likeness. We have the privilege of reflecting the image of our Creator and of having relationship with Him. But then sin entered the world and drove us to run *from* instead of *to* the Eternal Life Giver. We are hiding from the wrong thing.

The Bible tells us that without Christ we are "dead in sin" (see

Colossians 2:13). There is a vivid picture from Virgil's account of ancient history that might help you grasp what this means. It is said that Etruscan king Mezentius attached dead bodies to his living captives. Imagine carrying a dead body around. Over the weeks, as the putrefying body decomposed, constant contact with dead flesh caused the living, healthy skin to also begin to disintegrate. Because of his close contact with the corpse, the living man became, in essence, a walking dead man.[2] Without Christ, that is who we are.

The apostle Paul referred to a more deeply rooted evil when he cried from the depths of his being, "What a wretched man I am! Who will rescue me from this body of death?" (Romans 7:24). When the wreck of our lives or the lives of those we love overwhelms us and we realize we do not have what it takes to be free from the sin and ugliness, hopelessness can overcome us. That's how Betty felt. Do you feel that way? If so, we have good news for you.

God's plan from eternity was to *redeem* us from the Fall. In response to God's plan, which answers Paul's question of who can free us from sin, the apostle wrote,

> *The answer, thank God, is that Jesus Christ . . . does. He acted to set things right in this life of contradictions where I want to serve God with all my heart and mind, but am pulled by the influence of sin to do something totally different. . . . With the arrival of Jesus, the Messiah, that fateful dilemma is resolved. . . . A new power is in operation. The Spirit of life in Christ, like a strong wind, has magnificently cleared the air, freeing you from a fated lifetime of brutal tyranny at the hands of sin and death. God . . . didn't deal with the problem as something remote and unimportant. In his Son, Jesus, he personally took on the human condition, entered the disordered mess of struggling humanity in order to set it right once and for all. (Romans 7:25; 8:1-3, MSG)*

In other words, Jesus is our Kinsman-Redeemer. He came to set us free.

Our Kinsman-Redeemer

In the Old Testament, which is where we first see the concept of redemption, a redeemer was someone who restored another person and put things back into their original or pristine condition. A kinsman-redeemer was a relative who had an influential position either financially or socially and was willing to assume responsibility to provide for a helpless family member.

Mimi:

Years ago my husband and I were able to be kinsman-redeemers for my brother in-law and sister-in-law, who were in a horrible car accident halfway around the world. The family asked if my mother-in-law, Cal, and I would go to the hospital, assess the situation, and bring our relatives home. So that's what we did. When we walked into their hospital room, my bandaged and bruised brother-in-law wept for joy. He knew that we had come to cancel their medical bills and take him and his wife home. As kinsman-redeemers, we had the money, the authority, and, most of all, the love to accomplish that daunting task.

God's plan all along was to send Jesus, *our* Kinsman-Redeemer, to earth to redeem us with the price of His own blood. "It was . . . with the precious blood of Christ, a lamb without blemish or defect. He was chosen before the creation of the world" (1 Peter 1:18-20). God knew about sin and its profound devastation before Adam and Eve even fell into it. The Fall did not catch Him by surprise. He set the cure in motion before the illness began.

Before our new birth in Christ, we could be good, but no human goodness can gain us relationship with a Holy God (see Isaiah 64:6), let alone make us fit for Him to live in us. It would be like trying to use an American hair dryer in Europe. It looks like everybody else's, but it won't work because it can handle only 110 volts. Because the European electrical standard is 220 volts, our hair dryer will burn up when we plug it in and turn it on. Similarly, if we tried to relate to God based on our own goodness, God's holiness would instantly burn up our inner "circuits." We need new "wiring" to be able to house the Spirit of the living God. It is only by receiving God's goodness through Jesus Christ that we can enjoy relationship with Him. The old "wiring" — our unredeemed goodness — would not be able to handle God's power. Because of Jesus' death and resurrection, we can enjoy God's divine presence within us and not burn up with His holiness. We can choose not to sin — to be dead to it — and that gives hope. We like how Dallas Willard describes it:

> To be dead to sin with Christ is not to be lacking in these natural desires, but to have a real alternative to sin. . . . In our new life, we are capable of standing beyond sin's reach as we choose what we will do, and in that sense we are unattached from it — we are dead to it. We have a new force with us that gives us choice. In this sense we are free from sin even if not yet free of it.[3]

Redeeming Our Past

If despair is caused by our own sinful choices, the key to opening up the new life God wants to give us lies in our past. We may be ashamed or embarrassed to acknowledge the ugly things that lie behind us; we may not want to think of them because they hurt too much. God wants to use them in order to open up our present and future. We know because that is exactly how He worked in Mimi's life.

Mimi:

My soul was weary. I had lost interest in life. It felt as though I were hauling a big bag of trash from one day to the next. I didn't dare put it down because there were things in my past that were too painful for me to think about, let alone let go of. I thought I could "handle" it as long as it was contained. It seemed as if every day I dragged more and more weight around in my inner life. The older I got, the more stuff there was to deal with and the less weight I could carry. I didn't realize that God wanted to use the pain of my past to provide for my future. I finally began to address my problem by asking God to help me want Him to reveal the hidden spots of ugliness in my heart.

I came to the place where I brought my past into the present and laid it out before God with all its regrets and raw wounds. The ache of being different from other students, harsh memories from years spent in boarding school, hurtful remarks teachers had made about my dyslexia, and missing out on family life during my teen years were just some of the many painful things I placed before God.

I had to ask His forgiveness for my part in many of the painful memories. For the part others had played, I had to ask Him to forgive through me because I had been hurt so deeply. I knew that I did not have enough forgiveness in the bank of my soul to make the moment-by-moment withdrawals necessary to cover the pain. He never asks us to make a withdrawal if He has not made a deposit. I asked God to love through me into that hurtful memory. I learned that by choosing to forgive with His help, I didn't have to wait for my re-creation process to be completed to be free of the weight of the pain. I could be lighthearted as God continued His work in me.

Many of my past wounds resulted from the struggle of trying to articulate what is going on in my head and not being able to. That combined with knowing deep loneliness could have scarred me irreparably. But as God did His re-creation work in me, what had been grief turned to compassion and understanding. I know something of the isolation and struggle that someone who is hearing impaired or physically challenged experiences. Through His re-creation, God freed me to turn and pour love from my healed heart and spend my re-created energies on my world.

Mimi worked tirelessly to create a program for the hearing impaired and physically challenged in Ecuador. Countless numbers of people who had no hope of help before are receiving education, learning marketable skills, and being encouraged because one woman was determined not to carry her pain and instead let God use it to re-create her. She cooperated with God to make her grief the springboard for great things.

Perhaps you're thinking, *Sure, Christ can make things new for Mimi. But I just can't erase the scars and ugliness from my past. Haven't those things ruined me for God's best? Can He re-create the junk behind me?* Isaiah 52:12 tells us, "The Lord will go before you, the God of Israel will be your rear guard." When an army goes into new territory, it often sends advance troops — a vanguard — as well as a rear guard to defend the soldiers' backs. The rear guard also has the responsibility to pick up anything left behind.

There is a beautiful and tender meaning in the concept of the rear guard that gives us comfort. God uses these two words to describe His loving work. The Lord is our Vanguard and our Rear Guard. He follows behind not only to defend us should the Enemy attack from the back but also to help us when we lag and are weary. He gathers up the things we have dropped — our broken dreams, hurts, failed resolutions, mistakes, everything — and takes care of them Himself.

Can you see God's eternal goodness, love, and tenderness in this concept? As we allow Him to deal with our past, the poison of the memories begins to ease. Soon we can remember without the familiar jab of pain. God transforms the things that have caused us grief and makes them into useful, good things. "Redemption promises not replacement — a wholly new creation imposed on the old — but a transformation that somehow makes use of all that went on before. . . . In the end evil will serve as a tool of good."[4]

God wants to use the evil that has happened to us as a tool for good. He doesn't remove the evil; He redeems it and re-creates it. He transforms our personal disaster into something full of life and value. Philip Yancey says, "It should not surprise us that a sovereign God uses bad things as raw material for fashioning good."[5]

A few years ago, a friend from Africa came to visit and gave us a picture of what our Re-Creator does with us. As she was unpacking, she pulled a beautiful handmade necklace out of her suitcase. It was unique and remarkable. She said that women dig through the garbage and refuse near her home and then take pieces of trash and out of it create something lovely.

God has done exactly this with our friend Lynn. She grew up in a conservative, warm, loving home, the daughter of a wonderful pastor and his wife. However, Lynn was sure she was missing a lot of fun because of the narrow views of her parents. When she was in high school, she began sneaking out to parties and getting drunk. One night while Lynn was in a drunken stupor, she was raped and became pregnant. She was scared to death. She didn't want her parents to find out what kind of life she was leading, so she had an abortion. She pushed the thoughts and painful memories aside and threw herself into having a good time.

She went to a Christian college because her parents expected her to. There she fell in love with a nice man who wanted to be a preacher. She laughed inside at the thought of being a pastor's wife — if anybody knew what she was hiding! She didn't even tell her fiancé.

After they married, Lynn worked hard on her relationship with God but became consumed with terror that someday everyone would figure out that she was a fake. She turned into everything a pastor's wife shouldn't be: gossipy, jealous, vindictive, judgmental, exclusive, and proud, while desperately trying to hide from herself as well as everyone else.

Lynn had been living with the destruction of her secret past for almost fifteen years when we introduced the Creator/Redeemer/Re-Creator principles to her. That was years ago. The change in her is amazing. She will tell you that when she finally laid all of her past and scars before God and let Him begin the re-creation process, she was able to confess it to her husband. Out of her spiritual freedom, she began to live transparently in her re-creation while waiting patiently for her husband to be able to forgive her.

Today Lynn is a biblical counselor who has a life-changing ministry with broken and damaged teens. She tells them that she has walked where they walk. Her impact on them is profound because she is a vivid example that God can take the shattered pieces of a life and re-create them into beauty, joy, and significance.

Our Creator God is remaking us, forming in us a life that never existed before. We are so used to copying goodness. We think that is the message of Christianity, but God is not a copier. "If anyone is in Christ, he is a *new creation*; the old has gone, the new has come!" (2 Corinthians 5:17, emphasis added). *New* in this verse refers not only to something recently produced but also to one whose likeness has never existed. Our new life bears the glorious title "Christ's One." We are re-created. We pulsate with Christ's life.

New Life

God's purpose in redemption was to give us new life. He wants to comfort us in our despair and give us rebirth. He alone has the power to do this. Our Creator God, who is able to create something out of nothing, is able to make *all* things new.

The thing life is fullest of is the thing we find hardest to believe in. New beginnings. The incredible gift of a fresh start. Every new year. Every new day. Every new life. What wonderful gifts! And when we spoil things and life goes all wrong, we feel dismayed because we feel it is too hard to see that we can start again. . . . Only God can give life . . . make a baby or a new year.[6]

Because of Him, we have hope — hope of redemption, rebirth, and re-creation.

We opened this chapter with Betty's story. We wish we could end it by telling you that Betty and her husband are living happily ever after, but they're not. They are separated, although they are working toward reconciliation. Her sons continue living sinful lives. But Betty has not allowed the wrong choices of those she loves to keep her from experiencing God's good hand in her life. She came to understand the truth in 2 Corinthians 4:16-18:

Even though on the outside it often looks like things are falling apart on us, on the inside, where God is making new life, not a day goes by without his unfolding grace. These hard times are small potatoes. . . . There's far more here than meets the eye. The things we see now are here today, gone tomorrow. But the things *we can't see* now *will last forever.* (MSG, emphasis added)

Betty told both of us, "I never could have made it if it weren't for the Creator/Redeemer/Re-Creator concept. He has given me joy in spite of the destruction of my dreams. And He's using me!" Grieving mothers call her to pray with them and talk about their difficult children because she knows what they are facing. Other women look regularly to Betty for advice, spiritual encouragement, grace, and wisdom as they deal with their husband's deceitfulness and addictions to sex and pornography. When we first met Betty, pain was sucking the life out of her heart and body. Now, however, the shipwreck of her marriage and family has become life for many others as Betty has gone beyond the truth that God created and redeemed her and taken hold of God's re-creation. He is making her re-created life a thing of beauty.

Lord, we praise You because You are our good Creator God. We honor You for Your plan to redeem us from sin and death. Make us sensitive to how the pain and wounding we carry from one day to the next weigh us down. Thank You that You not only forgive us our sins but also re-create us. Thank You for taking the ugliness of our past, picking it up, and making the wrong things we've done be the first note of a new song. May the song that we are now glorify You in every way.

Holy Habits

- Verse to memorize: "If anyone is in Christ, he is a new creation; the old has gone, the new has come!" (2 Corinthians 5:17).

- Find something that would be valueless except for the fact that it has had a purpose change (a cracked teapot turned flowerpot, a broken ladder turned quilt display, an old-fashioned iron turned doorstop). Display it so that when you see it, you thank God that He is re-creating you, using your past as the raw material for something beautiful.

- Each time you plug in a small appliance you use regularly (a hair dryer, toaster, coffeepot, and so on), thank God that it is not your goodness that makes it possible for you to contain His Spirit but that it is because of Jesus' blood that you can enjoy relationship with Him and not burn up.

- When you throw something away, remind yourself that there is nothing God can't use in your life. Breathe a quick prayer, thanking Him for not wasting anything in your life.

- When you listen to a news broadcast or watch it on television, ask God to help you see it through the redemption He offers on the cross. For example, when you hear of the arrest of a child molester, pray that the perpetrator will let God redeem and re-create him. Pray that the wounded little one will know the re-creation of God and His healing.

Responding to His Word

1. In Job 38:4-7, read God's words about the act of Creation. What do you think Creation looked and sounded like?
2. Read Ezekiel 36:26; 2 Corinthians 5:17; Ephesians 4:24. How are God's promises in the Old Testament met by what He says in the New Testament?
3. The following verses, among others, give us some idea of what our Creator/Redeemer/Re-Creator is like: Psalm 19:14; Proverbs 23:11; Isaiah 41:14; 44:24; Jeremiah 50:34. Make a list of what you learn about Him from these passages.
4. Study 2 Peter 1:5-9. Note that verse 5 begins with, "For this very reason . . ." Peter is referring to what God said in the previous verses. In light of what God has provided, what does Peter encourage you to do?
5. According to 2 Peter 1:5-9, what will be the result of the outworking of these qualities in your life?
6. Re-creation means being made new. Study Titus 3:5; James 1:18; 1 Peter 1:3-4,23. From what the verses teach, write a paragraph expressing what you understand about being made new.
7. How does the promise in Romans 8:28-29 relate to re-creation?

8. What does John 3:3 tell us that the born-again will see? What do you understand that to mean? What would not seeing it mean?

9. Why is Romans 8:1-4 so important for the Creator/Redeemer/Re-Creator concept?

10. What truth from this chapter has affected you the most? What difference will it make in how you see yourself and God this week?

Chapter 11

Expecting Him to Show Up

Bombs exploded and gunfire split the night just outside Heather Mercer's window. In 2001, she and her friend Dana Curry had been hostages of the Taliban in Afghanistan. Now she was in Iraq, once again fearing for her life. Shaking with terror, Heather dove under her bed. *Am I going to die? I'm all alone!* she thought as the floor shook from the force of the nearby explosions. It was pitch-dark; she could not see her hand in front of her face. "Jesus," she whispered, "would You come and lie down under my bed next to me and be my Friend?" Then she felt something. "Jesus came and lay next to me. He was my Friend!"[1] she told a riveted audience several months after the incident.

Most of us have never dodged bombs and bullets, but many of us do know deep fear, helplessness, and aloneness. A lot of us are "hiding under the bed" from the battle of life, and we feel so alone. No matter how stinky and miserable a situation we find ourselves in, God is with us. And when we look for Him, He shows up.

Shadrach, Meshach, and Abednego knew about God's presence in the middle of a painful situation (see Daniel 3). The three of them were thrown fully clothed and firmly tied up into a furnace heated seven times hotter than usual, yet only the ropes tying them were burned. But the most amazing part is that observers saw a fourth man with them in the fire. God was so near that He actually walked with these three godly men in the blazing furnace.

When they came out of the fire, the fourth man was gone. What a mixture of feelings the three men must have experienced. They were out of the deadly situation, but God's presence was no longer palpable. That does not have to happen today. God's residence within us means He doesn't retreat after a crisis has passed. He lives with us. Whether you feel Him or not, because you are a child of God, His presence is always with you. There is *never* a time when you are without Him.

A Long History of Dwelling with Us

God first came to be with humankind in the Garden of Eden, the place He had specially designed for Adam and Eve. It was paradise. Paradise equals intimacy with Him. Christ told the thief on the cross, "Today you will be *with me*" (Luke 23:43, emphasis added). Most of us look for the ideal life outside of God, but He created us to be with Him — true paradise.

When sin came into the garden, humankind became distanced from God and could no longer live in paradise. Immediately we see the transcendent goodness of God as He introduced the sacrificial system so the Israelites could receive forgiveness of sin and maintain an ongoing relationship with Him. When the Israelites wandered in the desert, His presence was with them in a pillar of cloud by day and a pillar of fire by night.

Then He dwelt in the tabernacle they built in the center of the Israelite camp. God wanted to be as near to them as His holiness would permit. At the tabernacle's dedication, God's presence so filled the place, Moses could not enter it (see Exodus 40:34).

In that portable temple, God's presence was mostly confined to a place called the Holy of Holies, which was separated from the rest of the worship area by a thick, heavy curtain (see 26:33). It was so sacred that only the high priest could go in once a year, and he had to go through special preparations for the event. He had a rope tied to him so that if anything happened, the other priests could pull him out. No one other than the specially prepared high priest could go into God's presence without being struck dead. Silence and fear gripped those waiting outside while the high priest performed his duties in the Holy of Holies.

When the children of Israel settled in the Promised Land, Solomon built a temple so they could worship God and offer sacrifices. When it was dedicated, all the musicians praised God, singing, "He is good; his love endures forever" (2 Chronicles 5:13). As they sang, God's presence so filled the area that the priests could not carry out their duties.

Where God Lives Today

Jesus made it possible for us to know the personal presence of God in a way the Israelites never knew. The moment He died, the curtain that separated God's terrifying presence from the rest of the temple (and from the people) was torn from top to bottom, representing that because of Jesus we now have free, joyful access into the most holy place (see Matthew 27:51). Because of Christ's sacrifice, we can all come near to God.

Peter tells us, "You are a chosen people, a royal priesthood, a holy nation, a people belonging to God, that you may declare the praises of him who called you out of darkness into his marvelous light" (1 Peter 2:9). As a believer, you are the high priest of your heart. The Bible also tells us that when Christ put His Spirit within you, you became "the temple of the living God" (2 Corinthians 6:16). He placed the Holy of Holies within the heart of everyone who believes in Him. God lives in you. There is never a time when you are without Him. This relationship is for you to enjoy for now and eternity. Sit with that truth for a bit. Let the wonder of it sink deep within you and stir your heart.

How Practicing His Presence Changes Us

St. Bernard of Clairvaux wrote this about how God's presence changed his life:

> *[God] entered . . . not by the eyes for His presence was not marked by color; Nor by the ears, for there was no sound; Nor by the breath, for He mingled with the air; Nor by the touch, for He was impalpable. You ask then how I knew that He was present. Because He was a quickening [living Spirit] power. As soon as He entered, He awakened my slumbering soul. He moved and pierced my heart, which before was strange, stony, hard and sick.*[2]

When we delight in His presence, it is a transformational, God-centered existence.

We're never without His perspective. When we practice His presence, it changes how we view life. The awareness of God's indwelling Spirit can help us realize that we are stewards of what He has given us. When we don't understand God's perspective, we think of everything as ours: my children, my husband, my parents, my dishes, my talents, my money, my car, my house, and the list goes on. An awareness of His residence within us changes that. We learn to care for our children because they are God's gift to us. Material things become merely tools to work with, not resources to store up. We discover that we are only stewards of our homes, cars, and closets. When we recognize that all of our money belongs to Him, it frees us financially. It is not 90 percent ours and 10 percent His; it is *all* His. We are simply the managers of the gifts. Have you ever noticed that God's promise that His presence will never leave or forsake us is in the context of challenging us on our dependence on money and what we have to be content (see Hebrews 13:5)? His presence gives us His perspective. We own nothing; everything we have God has given to us.

When we follow His direction regarding the use of what He has entrusted to us, we learn how to trust Him for future provision. Our prayer becomes, *Dear Lord, use all that we have — money, talents, energy, material goods, and ideas — in a way that brings You pleasure.*

We're never without His comfort. God's promise to always be with us provides us with the comfort of His presence. Often He meets our needs with a special "gift": a phone call from a dear friend just when we need a pick-me-up, a card in the mail, a hug from a friend, the smile of a stranger.

The two of us often tell God what we need, including comfort when we go to bed at night ("He gives to His beloved even in [her] sleep" [Psalm 127:2, NASB]) or when we are missing loved ones.

Mimi:

For five years, Cal and I lived in Jordan, thousands of miles away from our children and grandchildren. I desperately missed being near those precious little ones. Sometimes my longing was a physical ache.

One day I was in an airport and saw a young woman shrouded in a Burka. I was drawn to her by the way she held her baby close to her heart. She hugged her wrapped bundle with all the tenderness possible. I walked up to her, touched the edge of the baby's soft blanket, and said, "This is your treasure, isn't it?" She told me in perfect English that she had gone through four in vitro fertilizations before she was able to conceive her little boy. Then she reached out and placed her tiny darling in my arms. She had no idea what her gesture meant to me. I gently kissed the soft cheeks and, with tears of joy, rejoiced with her in the tiny little person I held. Only my indwelling Lord knew I had been aching for a "grandma fix."

As I left the airport that afternoon, my soul could hardly contain my joy. I had not told anyone of my longing, but deep within me the Spirit of God heard my heart. He had caused me to laugh in His gracious presence.

Never without His resident wisdom. Because He is wisdom and lives in us, we can access it whenever we need it. That's why James 1:5 is so significant: "If any of you lacks wisdom, he should ask God, who gives generously to all without finding fault, and it will be given to him." Not only does God provide wisdom generously, He doesn't find fault with us when we ask for it.

Many times women share their deep needs and heartaches with us. Often they ask us for counsel and advice and we don't know what to say. Has that happened to you? We may not have answers, but we know that God, who lives within us, does. As others pour out their hearts, we pray, *Give me wisdom, Lord. What's Your perspective on her situation? How can I encourage her? How can I help her draw closer to You?* We are always awed at what He gives to us to pass on to others when we are still and seek His wisdom.

Jesus came from the heart of the Father so we could know the inner counsel of God. Jesus was talking about Himself when He said, "The only begotten God who is in the bosom of the Father, He has explained Him" (John 1:18, NASB). A "bosom friend" is one who knows the secrets of your heart. In the intimacy of prayer, Jesus said, "Righteous Father . . . I have made you known to them, and will continue to make you known in order that the love you have for me may be *in them* and that I myself may be in them" (John 17:25-26, emphasis added). Jesus, who knows all that is in God's heart, came so that we could know His resident wisdom in us.

He is not just a companion but a soul mate. God's being *in* us is far more than companionship. When we live in awareness of His presence in us, He becomes the definition of soul mate.

A. W. Tozer describes it this way:

The fellowship of God is delightful beyond all telling. He communes with His redeemed ones in an easy, uninhibited fellowship that is restful and healing to the soul. He is not sensitive or selfish nor temperamental. What He is today we shall find Him tomorrow.... He is not hard to please.... He expects of us only what He has Himself first supplied. He is quick to mark every simple effort to please Him, and just as quick to overlook imperfections when He knows we meant to do His will. He loves us for ourselves and values our love more than galaxies of new created worlds.[3]

Despite these wonderful benefits, we can go days and weeks without being aware of God's presence within us. Why is that?

What Keeps Us From Practicing His Presence?

Unconfessed sin. When we are conscious of unconfessed sin, it can keep us from experiencing His presence. That is not because God removes Himself; it is because we run away. That's what Adam and Eve did. They ran from God when they sinned. When we try to entertain sin in the same place where God lives, we are "dancing with the Devil." We will deny God's presence within us, or at least ignore His voice, when we know that we are doing things that do not honor Him.

Wrong beliefs about God. Another deterrent to practicing His presence is what we believe about God. If we don't believe that He is good, that He loves us and is committed to us, we won't trust Him. Why would we want to be with someone to whom we cannot trust our lives? Throughout this book, we have addressed some of the more common areas that people struggle with when it comes to trusting Him enough to want His presence.

Dulled awareness and boredom. A universal problem in our day and age is dulled awareness, even boredom. *The Washington Post* did an experiment with Josh Bell, a world-class violinist. They asked him to dress like a street musician and play his virtually priceless Stradivarius in the Washington DC subway. He chose six of the best compositions ever written for the violin. Passersby were treated to the top violinist playing the finest violin while performing the greatest music. Josh Bell stood near the escalator and played for forty-three minutes.

Three days before he posed as a street musician, the famous violinist had filled Boston's Symphony Hall, where tickets for good seats cost a hundred dollars. One thousand ninety-seven people walked by as the majestic music filled the subway. One stopped for more than a minute and only one stayed longer.[4] Two weeks after the subway concert, Josh Bell played for a standing-room-only crowd at the Music Center in North Bethesda, Maryland.

The Washington Post experiment shows how unaware we can be. The King of kings and Lord of lords is ever-present within us, but many of us, such as the passersby in the Washington subway, don't realize what is available to us.

Not expecting Him. The following story shows some of the other things that keep us from recognizing His presence. Jesus had freed Mary Magdalene from the bondage of seven demons (see Luke 8:2), and she loved Him very much. When He died, she wanted to do nothing more than be near His grave. But from sundown on Friday to sundown on Saturday, the Sabbath laws restricted her travel and she could go only a short distance from her home. That's why we find her at the tomb very early on Sunday morning before daylight. She went as soon as she could to be near the body of her Lord.

When she arrived at the place where Jesus was buried, she found the stone rolled away. She quickly ran to tell the apostles and then followed them back to the burial site. After the disciples went home, Mary stayed; her heart was heavy. It was then that Jesus showed up. But she didn't recognize Him (see John 20:14). She didn't see Him because she wasn't expecting Him. Sometimes we too fail to recognize Him because we don't expect Him to show up. We are so used to doing things on our own that we forget to invite Him to participate, and even when we do, we don't really expect that He will do anything.

Looking in the wrong place. She also missed Him because she was looking in the wrong place. She was bent over, looking in the tomb (see John 20:10). We too look for His presence in the wrong places. We think that God has to answer our prayers or respond in a certain way, maybe through a particular individual, place, or event. We think we know what's best for us and expect Him to come through according to what we want.

Focused on the wrong thing. Because she was weeping, Mary didn't realize Jesus was there. She was focused on her grief, tears blinding her eyes. Like Mary, we might focus on our pain and agony, which can keep us from being aware of God's continual presence.

Shelly:

During a recent crisis, I had to battle to keep focused on the presence of God because pain and grief kept clouding my heart and mind. I had to continually remind myself that the events did not catch God by surprise—He knew. When the darkness and heaviness closed in and I didn't feel He was anywhere near, I chose with my will to praise Him. I clung to the truth in Psalm 22:3, "He inhabits the praises of His people" (my paraphrase). As I praised Him with my will for everything that came to mind, including the crisis, I began to become conscious of His presence once again.

The Blessing of His Presence

Mary Magdalene recognized Jesus when He said her name, "Mary." She had probably never heard her name expressed more tenderly. During His time on earth, Jesus said, "My sheep listen to my voice; I know them" (John 10:27). Mary knew His voice and threw her arms around her Master. He gave her a message to take back to the others. She was to tell them, "I have seen the Lord!" (20:18).

Jesus gave Mary an extraordinary responsibility. Women were

considered to be the lowest class of human beings, barely above the animals. Every morning, the Pharisees thanked God that He had not made them a woman. The resurrected Christ showed Himself first to a woman and then gave her the joyful responsibility of announcing His resurrection to His disciples. But Mary nearly missed it.

Our friends Luke and Rose had a brand-new baby. They had missed church for several Sundays and could hardly wait to see their friends. The first Sunday back, they put their newborn in the nursery. After church they stood around chatting and reconnecting with everyone and then got in their car and headed home. They were a block away before they realized that the car seat was empty. Stunned, Rose exclaimed, "We forgot the baby!"

These new parents needed to practice an awareness of their baby's presence. This required a change of lifestyle and changes in their activities and thinking. We might not be able to imagine forgetting a new baby, but we often fail to practice God's presence and leave Him out of our lives.

So how do we learn to practice God's presence?

Practicing His Presence

The expression "Practice the presence" gives us a clue as to how to go about being aware of God's presence within us. We have to practice — work at — a consciousness of His residence within us. We're not talking about a bunch of holy habits strung together but about a lifestyle of developing an awareness of His presence.

Brother Lawrence was a seventeenth-century monk who spent his life serving God in the kitchen. He made it his life's goal to live continually in God's presence. He said,

The time of business does not, with me, differ from the time of prayer. And in the noise and clatter of my kitchen, while several persons are

at the same time calling for different things, I possess God in as great tranquility as if I were on my knees. . . . I make it my business only to persevere in His Holy presence wherein I keep myself by a simple attention and an habitual, silent and secret conversation of the soul with God.[5]

The two of us practice His presence by greeting Him when we wake and talking to Him throughout the day. We each consult Him on decisions all day long, asking, "Lord, what would be best? What do You want me to do?" We listen for His counsel in our hearts and look for evidence of His hand in our daily events. At times, we set an alarm for 8 a.m., 10 a.m., noon, 2 p.m., and so on as simple reminders to check how we're doing in remembering and acknowledging Him in our activities.

It's easy to be hard on ourselves if the alarm goes off mid-morning and we realize that we haven't thought of the Lord since it rang two hours ago. We can get frustrated and become preoccupied by the fact that we've been distracted. Then several hours later we wake up to the fact that we've wasted another two hours beating ourselves up for forgetting His presence, and by then we are ready to give up trying!

God is not offended by our humanness. He made us and He knows that we get distracted. Satan would like nothing better than for us to be so preoccupied with not practicing the presence of God that we don't do it! All we need to do when we've forgotten that He's with us is turn our hearts toward Him and announce, "I'm back!" A. W. Tozer says,

How good it would be if we could learn that God is easy to live with. He remembers our frame and knows that we are dust. He may sometimes chasten us, it is true, but even this He does with a smile, the proud, tender smile of a Father who is bursting with pleasure over an imperfect but promising son who is coming every day to look more and more like the One whose child he is.[6]

The result of practicing an ever-growing awareness of His presence is that we become more and more like Jesus.

The holy habits we suggest at the end of each chapter in this book are all ways to help you to remind yourself to pay daily attention to God's presence in your life and work. When we practice His presence, we can know with delight that He is there, even when we're on our knees scrubbing the toilet, washing pots and pans, changing diapers, writing a report, or commuting to and from work.

When you live in the circle of God's goodness, you can enjoy the wonder that you aren't alone, that He is always with you. You can delight in His indwelling presence. When you do that, you will not take His presence for granted but savor it, never wanting to leave. You are never without resident wisdom, because God is Wisdom (see Romans 11:33). You are never without comfort, because He is the God of all comfort (see 2 Corinthians 1:3). Because He lives in you, you are never without an eternal perspective; He is Eternal and has given you the mind of Christ (see 1 Corinthians 2:16) for you to enjoy for now and eternity.

Gracious One, how can we ever thank You for free access to Your presence? You thought of this plan before the world was born. We bow low in Your presence and kiss Your hand (see Psalm 2:12) because You brought this to be. We love You. May we grow daily more conscious of Your holy residence within us. We ask that Your presence dance over the doors and windows of our homes. May You be evident at every turn.

Holy Habits

- Verse to memorize: "Blessed are those who have learned to acclaim you, who walk in the light of your presence, O Lord" (Psalm 89:15).

- Place an extra chair or set another place at the table when you sit down to eat. Let it remind you that God shares the meal with you. When you cultivate that consciousness, it can bring pleasure to everyday events. "Through our daily meals He is calling us to rejoice, to keep holiday in the midst of our working day."[7]

- Take a few minutes during your day to stop and become conscious of your breathing. Take a few deep breaths. Remember the words Michael W. Smith sings, "This Is the Air I Breathe"? As you slowly draw in air, ask God to allow you to be aware of how He fills the air around you. As you go through the day, ask God for what we call "princess moments." A princess moment is when the King of kings and Lord of lords shows you that you are His precious daughter and that He is with you. Such moments can be as simple as tasting a delicious plum or finding a great parking spot or as miraculous as receiving an unexpected inheritance or healing.

- Stop yourself throughout the day. Set an alarm if you have to. Offer each decision and joy, each sorrow and pleasure, to God as a love offering. Talk to Him as you go about your daily responsibilities. Discuss your concerns with Him, just as you would with your closest confidante.

- When you take your garbage out, check your heart. Ask yourself, *Is my heart empty of sin so I can freely enjoy God's presence?*

Responding to His Word

1. "The fear of the Lord" means the recognition of His power and His presence.[8] Read the following verses and list what God's presence provides: Proverbs 17:24; Acts 3:19; 2 Corinthians 5:1-10.

2. How can Psalm 31:19-20 be a reality in your life? (Remember the definition of the "fear of the Lord" from question 1.)

3. Read Matthew 18:20; 28:20; 1 John 3:24. List where and when God's presence is promised.

4. Read Daniel 3:13-27. How sure were Shadrach, Meshach, and Abednego of God's ability to care for them? How did they experience the presence of God? What was the result?

5. How does Isaiah 43:2 tell us that God's presence is evident? Note that the word *when* shows up twice in that verse. Why might that be important?

6. Is there anything that can separate you from His presence? Support what you believe, using verses of Scripture.

7. Read Acts 17:24-28. Using your own words, explain what Paul is saying about God's presence. How have you practiced an awareness of God's presence?

8. What does Colossians 1:27 tell us about Christ in us? What do you think that looks like in the life of a believer?

9. Read 2 Corinthians 6:14–7:1. What promises does 7:1 refer to? What things do we need to do in order to be God's temple?

10. Identify the truths from 2 Corinthians 6:14–7:1 that can motivate you to do the things you listed in question 9.

Chapter 12

Enjoying His Rest

After spending ten years studying the goodness of God, it feels as if we've only scratched the surface. Choosing to live in the circle of God's goodness has grown our faith and joy. As we continually learn to rest in His goodness, He has also prepared us to face new challenges.

Mimi:

When I began to study the goodness of God, I had no idea what lay ahead. For most of my life, I have been very healthy. I have hardly spent a day in bed. It's amazing in light of the many places we've traveled and all of the virulent germs I've been exposed to.

But several years ago, things began to change. I started to notice that my body was slowing down. I have always moved quickly and had a lot of energy, but my walk slowed dramatically. Even when I tried to speed up, I couldn't. My right hand shook slightly, and it became increasingly difficult to write notes. Letters that had once easily flowed from my pen now took extra time and care so that I could write legibly. People often tell me that they can barely see, let alone read, my writing.

I am a nurse and my husband, Cal, is a doctor, so I knew enough to suspect Parkinson's disease. But months would go by without any symptoms, and I wondered if they had been my imagination. Then they would return more intensely. When I confided my concerns to the doctor, he told me that there were two possible causes: a brain tumor or Parkinson's disease. Neither option sounded good.

When the test results confirmed that I had Parkinson's, I felt like the air had been knocked out of me. I realized that I could continue to live intentionally, but now I had to include the reality of Parkinson's. Because I have practiced the presence of our good God for so long, I went right to His feet. My dyslexia makes me see everything in pictures, and the picture He gave me was the one we painted for you in chapter 1 of Eve in the garden. What would it have been like, I wondered, if Eve, when she was faced with the temptation to question God's goodness, had taken Satan up to a high place and asked him to look to the north, south, east, and west? She could have shown him that as far as his eye could see in a 360-degree circle, God had filled the garden with good things that she could eat and enjoy. So why would she sit under the tree she could not have? I asked myself the same question.

My answer is, my Father, in His wisdom and goodness, has made it clear that what I cannot have is life without Parkinson's. I will not camp under the tree I cannot have. When I lay God's presence, His indwelling Spirit, and His goodness onto my future with this debilitating illness, I can rest.

I have watched people with Parkinson's deteriorate, losing their abilities to walk, talk, and move normally, as well as to do other functions we usually take for granted. I know what lies ahead. I could be terrified when I think about the Parkinson's. But I am not. My body has Parkinson's disease, but my longing is to choose, moment by moment, not to allow it to infect my spirit.

Instead, I choose to practice the holy habit of living within God's absolute goodness in the present moment. Many times a day when my body reminds me of the debilitating disease and I am tempted *to wonder about tomorrow, I say to myself, I have today. This day is going to look very good when I reflect back on it five years from now.*

Because God is good, I am willing to face each day with Him, to wait and see what He has in mind. The verse that I repeat many times a day is, "Be at rest once more, O my soul, for the LORD has been good to you" (Psalm 116:7).

Mimi is choosing to let God carry the heaviness of the unknown; she is resting in the circle of His goodness.

Listen to God's sweet invitation, *"Come* to me, all you who are weary and burdened, and I will give you *rest.* Take my yoke upon you and learn from me, for I am gentle and humble in heart, and you will find *rest* for your souls. For my yoke is easy and my burden is light" (Matthew 11:28-30, emphasis added). God wants you to rest, to stop trying to manage your life outside of the circle of His goodness. He wants you to nestle into Him as you would a soft comfortable recliner. When you do, He will give you rest.

You can rest in the circle of His goodness because:

- **He is absolutely good.** "The LORD is good, a refuge in times of trouble. He cares for those who trust in him" (Nahum 1:7).
- **He is Light and will give you light.** "The commands of the LORD are radiant, giving light to the eyes" (Psalm 19:8).
- **He loves you.** "See what [an incredible] quality of love the Father has given (shown, bestowed on) us, that we should [be permitted to] be named and called and counted the children of God!" (1 John 3:1, AMP).
- **He is holy and can make you holy.** "You are to be holy to me because I, the LORD, am holy, and I have set you apart from the nations to be my own" (Leviticus 20:26).
- **He is joy.** "Do not grieve, for the joy of the LORD is your strength" (Nehemiah 8:10).

- **He is the Three in One.** "May the grace of the Lord Jesus Christ, and the love of God, and the fellowship of the Holy Spirit be with you all" (2 Corinthians 13:14). We enjoy the blessing of relationship with God the Father, God the Son, and God the Holy Spirit.
- **He is sovereign over everything,** including everything that pertains to you. "O LORD, God of our fathers, are you not the God who is in heaven? You rule over all the kingdoms of the nations. Power and might are in your hand, and no one can withstand you" (2 Chronicles 20:6).
- **He offers relationship and makes an unbreakable covenant with you.** "'Though the mountains be shaken and the hills be removed, yet my unfailing love for you will not be shaken nor my covenant of peace be removed,' says the LORD, who has compassion on you" (Isaiah 54:10).
- **He is your Re-Creator.** He wants to take the junk of your life and use it as the first note of a new song. "Forget the former things; do not dwell on the past. See, I am doing a new thing! Now it springs up; do you not perceive it? I am making a way in the desert and streams in the wasteland" (Isaiah 43:18-19).

This list fills us with wonder and awe. Our good God invites you to live in the middle of the goodness that He is. Don't let the thought of living in the circle of His goodness overwhelm you. You can choose to live in His goodness one day at a time.

Our friend Judi did the same while vigorously battling breast cancer for twelve years. Judi put a great deal of energy into being well. She lived on an extremely restricted diet, eating only vegetables and some natural chicken and fish. She ate no dairy and nothing artificial. She didn't put anything in her body that could possibly feed the cancer. She exercised faithfully, took large quantities of supplements, and fought hard to be healthy.

After winning several battles with the cancer, Judi went into hospice. Even though she was a private person, she opened up her heart and thoughts to her many friends worldwide through her e-mails, giving us the blessing and privilege of receiving profound insights into her journey as she faced death.

The following are Judi's thoughts on God's goodness, written a few short weeks before she died.

Perhaps it all began over fifty years ago when I memorized the Twenty-Third Psalm in Sunday school. . . . Verse 6 has been the one verse that I have struggled with as I've faced the certainty of a painful end of life. For decades I've gratefully received and embraced God's promises, but in recent years the assurance of His goodness following me all the days of my life just hasn't seemed to apply. Yet as one who professes no doubt in God's faithful Word, if I read between the lines of this seemingly unattainable promise, I can clearly see that He has promised He'll never turn His back on me, He'll never give up on me, He won't ever let me go, and He'll be absolutely relentless in His pursuit of me.

So how is this promise manifesting itself to me during these days? Once I got started on this list, it was hard to stop.

- *When I awaken each morning, I recognize His gracious gift of another day of life and breath in this beautiful state of Colorado.*
- *As I systematically pump more and more medication into my body throughout the day, I have a keen sense of His merciful desire to minimize my suffering.*
- *My heart leaps with the insistent ringing of the doorbell nearly every afternoon, assuring me of the love of a beloved daughter and two precious grandchildren who still get excited to traipse next door to Gamma's house.*

- *My husband is as loving a caregiver and chief prayer warrior as I could ever ask for.*
- *I have come to deeply love God's Word. It is comfort, sustenance, and truth to me.*
- *As I receive cards, e-mails, and visits from family and friends, I am tearfully grateful to the Lord for speaking so directly through them right to the heart of a current need. He hears and He speaks to me.*
- *When I go to bed each evening, He faithfully covers me with His wings and provides deep, restful, and uninterrupted sleep night after night.*
- *I do have one more amazing, and perhaps surprising, manifestation of His promise to relentlessly pursue and shower me with goodness during these days: My husband and I have always wanted to take our grandkids to Disneyland, and we decided that we might as well go for it. In the span of just one week, all the logistics have come together for us to take our daughter and four-year-old granddaughter to Disneyland. I'm requiring more care each day, but my indispensable hospice RN has pledged to work with us to get my increasing pain managed to the point where I'll be able to enjoy the trip (I hope without falling asleep on the roller-coaster!). And since I'll be using a wheelchair to get around, I've heard they move you to the front of the lines. Well, if that's not goodness and mercy! "Every good and perfect gift is from above" (James 1:17).*

As she faced a painful death, Judi chose to focus on God's goodness and found joy and rest. The morning Judi went to heaven, her husband Jack wrote,

Cancer was not the victor but was likely the strongest vehicle through which God chose to glorify Himself in Judi, despite her many talents and gifts. . . . The pain was extreme and difficult. Without minimizing the intensity of her suffering, as God so unmistakably displayed His power through her, the lessons we learned transcended the pain and were deep and life-changing.

One of the verses Judi shared with me in the days just before the morphine stole away her ability to communicate articulately . . . was this: (Jesus is speaking) "Now is your time of grief, but I will see you again and you will rejoice, and no one will take away your joy" (John 16:22).

Many of us, her friends and family, wondered why God would allow such a godly, beautiful, and gifted woman, with everything to live for, to face such pain and difficulty. We don't know why, but as Judi said, "We know Him." She learned the truth of Hebrews 12:26-27, where God says, "'Once more I will shake not only the earth but also the heavens.' The words 'once more' indicate the removing of what can be shaken — that is, created things — so that what cannot be shaken may remain." All Judi had left before she died was what could not be shaken. She could rest in the absolute assurance that God is who He said He is: He is good and He will keep His promises. Judi stepped into His eternal presence with that confidence. Now she knows the complete and full goodness of God.

You can too.

We have come to see that growing in our understanding of God's goodness is like building a sand dune with a handful of sand a day. Each day, you add a small amount of sand to the previous day's mound. Sometimes it feels as if not much is happening; days and weeks go by and there doesn't seem to be much to show for your daily deposit. Other times you might feel as though the sand gets blown away. But when you add to it every day, you will in time discover you have built a towering sand dune! One of Mimi's favorite phrases is "We have a lifetime to give to this." We don't know how long any of us has, but let's make it a lifelong goal to live in the circle of God's goodness.

Lord, we have tasted Your goodness. We praise You for opening it to us. We are awed that You surround us with who You are. Help us to step even farther into the circle of Your abundant goodness. We want to enjoy You and rest completely in who You are for every moment of our lives.

Holy Habits

- Verses to memorize: "Be at rest once more, O my soul, for the LORD has been good to you. For you, O LORD, have delivered my soul from death, my eyes from tears, my feet from stumbling" (Psalm 116:7-8).

- Communicate your celebration of the goodness of God. Listen to how you talk. From your words, what would the people around you say is your passion? If we want our children or others in our circle of influence to take up the celebration of the goodness of God where we leave off, our own lives need to reflect that ever-growing passion.

- As you fall asleep, ask God to waken people on the other side of the earth with a song of praise to Him so He receives continual praise. Mimi likes to worship in the late afternoon. During that time, she offers up worship on behalf of young mothers who are too busy with grumpy little ones and dinner preparation to worship. In turn, Mimi asks them to worship for her when they're up in the night with the children and she's sleeping. (We base this concept on Job's example of worshipping for his children [see Job 1:5]).

- Write out cards with words of Scripture, with truth about who God is and what He does. Put these cards where you will see them throughout your day: on the mirror, over the washing machine, on your computer monitor at work, on the sink where you wash dishes, on the dashboard of your car, and so on.

- Choose a favorite chair to be your "goodness of God" chair. Whenever you sit in it, relax fully into the chair, let it hold you, and say to Him, *Father, this is a physical manifestation of how I am choosing to hold nothing back. I am allowing all my weight to rest in Your goodness.*

- Plan to share with three people about the goodness of God this week. Make sure at least one of the three is younger than you are. Prepare what you will say and how you will say it. Remember that many people won't see the goodness of God unless someone points it out to them. Your example will teach others.

Responding to His Word

1. Read Moses' words to the Israelites in Deuteronomy 1:6-46. As you read, keep in mind that the Jews sometimes referred to entering the Promised Land as entering into rest.
2. Note all the things in that passage that show the attitudes of the children of Israel (for example, verse 28: looking elsewhere and not at God, blaming others, looking at man's perspective, comparisons, exaggerations, full of woe).
3. Go back through the passage and list what it says about who God is and what He wants to do.
4. Who does the passage say will enter the rest of the Promised Land and why?

5. What does this passage say to you about rest?
6. Read Psalm 145.
7. Note all the places where David makes an intentional statement.
8. List everything the psalm tells you about what God is and what He does.
9. Write a paragraph to God, responding to what David's words tell you about Him in Psalm 145.
10. What is the most significant lesson you have learned from this study?

Notes

Chapter 1: 360 Degrees of Absolute Goodness

1. Arthur W. Pink, *The Attributes of God* (Grand Rapids, MI: Baker, 1975), 57.
2. Matthew Henry, *Matthew Henry's Commentary on the Whole Bible* (Nashville: Nelson, 1997), Commentary on Romans 1:25.
3. John Wyeth and Robert Robinson, "Come Thou Fount of Every Blessing." Copyright by Paragon Associates, Inc., 1979.

Chapter 2: Out from Behind the Curtain

1. Reverend D. H. Kuiper, *The Independence or Self-Existence of God*, published by the Reformed Witness Committee, http://www.reformedwitness.org/pmphltlst/Attributes/Independence.html.
2. Dallas Willard, *True Spirituality: Transformed Living in Today's Culture,* Seminar, First Presbyterian Church, Colorado Springs, CO, March 11–12, 2005.

Chapter 3: Dancing in Life-Giving Light

1. NIV notes on Psalm 19:4-6.
2. The I Am's of Christ: The Messiah — John 4:26; The Bread of

Life — John 6:35; From Above — John 8:23; The Eternal One — John 8:58; The Door — John 10:7; The Son of God — John 10:36; The Resurrection and Life — John 11:25; The Lord and Master — John 13:13; The Way, Truth, and Life — John 14:6; The True Vine — John 15:1; Alpha and Omega — Revelation 1:8; The First and the Last — Revelation 1:17.

3. Bishop Fulton J. Sheen, *Life of Christ* (New York: Doubleday, 1953), 152.

4. Oswald Chambers, *The Complete Works of Oswald Chambers* (Grand Rapids, MI: Discovery House, 2000), 625.

5. http://en.wikipedia.org/wiki/Dark_Night_of_the_Soul.

Chapter 4: Swept Off Your Feet

1. Bishop Fulton J. Sheen, *Life of Christ* (New York: Doubleday, 1990), 222.

2. William Barclay, *The Daily Study Bible Series. The Letters to the Galatians and Ephesians* (Philadelphia: Westminster, 1976), 133.

3. A. W. Tozer, *The Knowledge of the Holy* (Lincoln, NE: Back to the Bible Broadcast, 1961), 109.

4. This chart is adapted from J. Sidlow Baxter, *For God So Loved: An In-Depth Look at the Bible's Most Loved Verse* (Grand Rapids, MI: Kregel, 1995), 57–58.

5. Oswald Chambers, *My Utmost for His Highest* (Grand Rapids, MI: Discovery House, 1992), February 4 reading.

6. Penelope Wilcock, *The Hawk and the Dove* (Wheaton, IL: Crossway, 2000), 333.

Chapter 5: Guilt-Free and Spiritually Whole

1. Associated Press report. October 5, 2005, http://www.msnbc .msn.com/id/9600151/.

2. Paul L. Maier, ed., *Josephus The Essential Works* (Grand Rapids, MI: Kregel, 1988), 172.

3. Revelation 4:6-8 also describes winged creatures.
4. David Needham with Larry Libby, "The Joy of Holiness," *Discipleship Journal*, Volume 9, January–February 1989, 39.
5. See 2 Corinthians 5:17; Galatians 6:15; Ephesians 4:22-25; 2 Peter 1:3.
6. A. W. Tozer, *The Root of Righteousness* (Camp Hill, PA: Wing Spread Publishers, 2006), 51.
7. Amy Carmichael, *Edges of His Ways* (London: Butler and Tanner Ltd., 1957), 100.

Chapter 6: Radiant with Joy

1. Mike Mason, *The Gospel According to Job* (Wheaton, IL: Crossway, 1994), 39.
2. Frederic Farrar, *The Life of Christ* (Portland, OR: Fountain Publications, 1976), Footnote on page 325.
3. Quoted by Bob Cargo: Audiocassette "On the Joy of the Lord," available on www.perimeter.org.
4. Leslie D. Weatherhead, quoted in Gordon S. Jackson, comp., *Quotes for the Journey, Wisdom for the Way* (Colorado Springs, CO: NavPress, 2000), 102.
5. G. K. Chesterton, *Orthodoxy* (Rockville, MD: Serenity Publishers, 2009), 61.
6. Weatherhead, 102.

Chapter 7: Becoming One

1. James Strong, ed., *The New Strong's Expanded Exhaustive Concordance of the Bible* (Nashville: Nelson, 2001), 50 of the Greek Dictionary of the New Testament.
2. Dallas Willard, *True Spirituality: Transformed Living in Today's Culture*, Seminar, First Presbyterian Church, Colorado Springs, CO, March 11–12, 2005.
3. Oswald Chambers, *My Utmost for His Highest* (Grand Rapids,

MI: Discovery House, 1992), March 3 reading.

4. Millard J. Erickson, *Making Sense of the Trinity* (Grand Rapids, MI: Baker, 2000), 60.

5. William P. Young, *The Shack* (Los Angeles: Windblown Media, 2007), 102.

6. Young, 101.

7. Young, 96.

8. Darrell W. Johnson, *Experiencing the Trinity* (Vancouver: Regent, 2002), 61.

9. Johnson, 78.

10. Cyprian Smith, *The Way of Paradox: Spiritual Life as Taught by Meister Eckhart* (London: Darton, Longman, and Todd, 1987), 10.

11. Johnson, 52.

12. Johnson, 60.

13. Johnson, 61.

Chapter 8: Trusting in His Grip

1. *Random House Webster's College Dictionary* (New York: Random House, 1999), 1253.

2. Oswald Chambers, *My Utmost for His Highest* (Grand Rapids, MI: Discovery House, 1992), May 8 reading.

Chapter 9: Beyond "Till Death Do Us Part"

1. James Strong, ed., *The New Strong's Expanded Exhaustive Concordance of the Bible* (Nashville: Nelson, 2001), 46 of The Hebrew and Aramaic Dictionary.

2. Stanley Grenz, David Guretzki, and Cherith Fee Nordling, *Pocket Dictionary of Theological Terms* (Downers Grove, IL: InterVarsity, 1999), 32.

3. Kevin Howard and Marvin Rosenthal, *The Feasts of the Lord* (Nashville: Nelson, 1997), 132.

4. Howard and Rosenthal, 131.
5. Pastor Steve Holt, Message at Mountain Springs Church, Colorado Springs, CO, January 29, 2006.

Chapter 10: Shipwrecks Turned Gorgeous Coral Reefs

1. Beth Moore, *Stepping Up: A Journey Through the Psalms of Ascent* (Nashville: LifeWay, 2007), 129.
2. F. F. Bruce, *Romans an Introduction and Commentary* (Carol Stream, IL: Tyndale, 2008), 155.
3. Dallas Willard, *The Spirit of the Disciplines: Understanding How God Changes Lives* (New York: HarperCollins, 1991), 115.
4. Philip Yancey, *Reaching for the Invisible God* (Grand Rapids, MI: Zondervan, 2000), 265.
5. Yancey, 261.
6. Penelope Wilcock, *The Hawk and the Dove* (Wheaton, IL: Crossway, 1991), 141.

Chapter 11: Expecting Him to Show Up

1. Heather Mercer, Message at Mission ConneXion Northwest, January 18, 2008.
2. F. B. Meyer, *Secret of Guidance* (Tappan, NJ: Fleming H. Revell, 1896), 107.
3. A. W. Tozer, *The Root of Righteousness* (Camp Hill, PA: Wing Spread Publishers, 1955), 13.
4. Gene Weingarten, "Pearls Before Breakfast," *The Washington Post*, April 8, 2007. Page W.10. www.washingtonpost.com/wp-dyn/content/article/2007/04/04/AR2007040401721.html
5. Brother Lawrence, *The Practice of the Presence of God* (Tappan, NJ: Fleming H. Revell, 1958), 8.
6. A. W. Tozer, 14.

7. Dietrich Bonhoeffer, *Light for My Path* (Uhrichsville, OH: Barbour, 1999), 104.
8. This principle was taught by Pastor Paul Steele of Valley Church in Cupertino, California.

About the Authors

Mimi was raised in the Belgian Congo and **Shelly** on the island of Taiwan. The two women met in Ecuador and have been friends and prayer partners for nearly a quarter of a century. Although they have studied the Bible for many years, nothing has influenced them more personally than the study of God's goodness. This understanding has increased their passion to know and demonstrate how the character of God can impact our daily lives. Shelly and Mimi both live in Colorado.

Become the woman
God created you to be.

Holy Habits
Mimi Wilson and Shelly Cook Volkhardt
978-1-57683-115-1

An intimate understanding of God lays the foundation for the changes you desire. Uncover this truth in the pages of *Holy Habits* as the authors reveal how their examination of the names of God enabled them to begin living intentionally. Includes a ten-week Bible study.

Dwelling in His Presence:
30 Days of Intimacy with God
Cynthia Heald
978-1-61521-024-4

In this insightful thirty-day devotional, best-selling author Cynthia Heald takes you into God's Word to explore His relentless, passionate pursuit of you. Day by day, you'll learn to listen and respond to the God who earnestly seeks you because He loves you. Each entry offers strong Bible teaching, personal stories, reflection questions, and action points that engage you in a truly transforming devotional experience.

Thirsty
Amy Nappa
978-1-60006-093-9

What does it look like to come into personal contact with Jesus? The woman at the well did, and He satisfied her thirst for living water. Meet Jesus at the well. Discover the gift of kindness and restoration that God has for you.

To order copies call NavPress at 1-800-366-7788
or log on to www.navpress.com.